Modernity and the Classical Tradition

Architectural Essays 1980–1987

Modernity and the Classical Tradition

Architectural Essays 1980–1987

Alan Colquhoun

The MIT Press
Cambridge, Massachusetts
London, England

First MIT Press paperback edition, 1991

©1989 Massachusetts Institute of Technology

This book was printed and bound in the United States of America.

Library of Congress Cataloging-in-Publication Data

Colquhoun, Alan, 1921–
    Modernity and the classical tradition : architectural essays,
1980–1987 / Alan Colquhoun.
      p. cm.
    Includes index.
    ISBN 0-262-03138-8 (hardcover)   0-262-53101-1 (paperback)
  1. Architecture and history. 2. Neoclassicism (Architecture)
  3. Functionalism (Architecture) 4. Architecture. Postmodern.
  I. Title.
NA2543.H55C65   1989   88-27270
724—dc19   CIP

Introduction

The essays collected in this book were written for different occasions and have no intentional thematic unity. Nonetheless, they tend to group themselves according to three different, but related, areas of interest. Those in the first section are concerned with some of the concepts that have dominated architectural discourse during the last two centuries and still to a large extent constitute the conceptual framework within which we "think architecture." The most important and at the same time the most ambiguous of these concepts is "history" itself. It is within the context of the changing meaning of "history" that all the "theories" of architecture have developed since the middle of the eighteenth century. Even today, the positions taken up by the various protagonists of the present architectural debate are based, explicitly or implicitly, on assumptions about the role of history in the formation of modern cultural values. This problem is addressed in the first four essays. The meanings of such key words as *classicism, romanticism, historicism,* and *rationalism* are discussed in relation not only to different time frames, but also to the varying conceptions of history on which they depend.

The essays in the second part of the book revolve around the same set of problems, but now seen in relation to the classical avant-garde—specifically the works of Le Corbusier, who, of all the masters of the modern movement, was the most acutely aware of the break in cultural continuity experienced in the early twentieth century. It is with the tensions and contradictions in his work that result from this, and from his attempt to mediate between the past and the present, that these three essays are mainly concerned.

The final section consists of essays in which current controversies are explicitly discussed, particularly the problem of so-called postmodernism. These are occasional essays in the fullest sense. Some are little more than sketches for more substantial essays that will never be written. Nevertheless, they perhaps have the effect of refocusing the earlier essays in the direction of our present predicament, showing their relevance to the present crisis.

The habit of talking about architecture in terms of "crisis" goes back to the end of the eighteenth century, when the classical tradition began to lose its exclusive authority and architects, with their newfound historical anxiety, began to look for alternative paradigms. The ensuing century suffered under two contradictory conceptions of history. The first held that history (defined as the representation of past events) provided models for imitation—a notion inherited from the eighteenth century and based on the traditional view that the purpose of historical studies was to learn from the past. The second conception saw history (now signifying the events themselves) as an irreversible process. Historical events owed their significance to the context in which they occurred, and it made no sense to treat any of these events as literal models. The only way to learn from the past was to try to discover the essential idea that lay behind the flux of events.

The "crisis" of architecture at the turn of the twentieth century was closely connected to the change from a practice based on the first conception of history to one based on the second. Whatever theoretical arguments were put forward in the course of the nineteenth century for a historicist interpretation of history and against the imitation of past styles, the practice of architecture, and the discourse connected with this practice, were still rooted in earlier habits of mind. There were, it is true, disagreements as to the way in which history should be used. Some said that different styles could be combined in the same work, others that only a single style should be followed. "Imitation" was interpreted differently, to mean the repetition of final forms or the discovery of underlying principles. But on one point all were agreed: the essence of architecture was to be found in historical examples.

All this changed toward the end of the nineteenth century, with the emergence of new practices that sought to establish other foundations for design than those of stylistic imitation and eclectic adaptation. These new avant-gardes operated between two polar extremes: that of a vitalistic, craft-oriented architecture and that of a rationalistic, machine-oriented architecture. They thus to some extent continued the romantic/classical argument that had characterized the nineteenth century. It was the second strand that became dominant in the post-World War I avant-garde and that set the tone of architectural practice as a whole after World War II.

Recently, critical attention has been refocused on the difference within the modern movement between those whose aim was to change the architectural language and those who had the more radical aim of destroying the institutional and professional framework of architecture by exposing the ideological basis of so-called architectural principles. Though this distinction is valid, it is nonetheless true that the great majority of architects in the modern movement were motivated by progressive social ideals. They saw their work in terms of a master narrative that provided them with a collective sense of purpose and a philosophical and social context within which to place architecture. It is the disappearance of this master narrative that is, perhaps, the most striking feature of the decline of the modernist ideology during the last two decades.

But one might postulate that a more generalized and less visible version of this master narrative had disappeared long before 1965—that according to which "history" provided the present with its sense of purpose. If this is so, one would have to provide a different interpretation of the roots of modernism from the one usually adopted. Historians of the modern movement, from Pevsner and Giedion to Benevolo, Collins, and Frampton, have always attempted to provide modernism with a genealogy, tracing its origins to some conjuncture of the nineteenth or even eighteenth century. In doing this they have been reinforcing the positivist notion that history is a continuous, coherent, and, on the whole, beneficial progression. It is true that the idea of progress that this historicist view propagates necessarily includes the idea of "newness." But it also implies that the present has grown out of the past on the analogy of biological evolution, and any reasonable interpretation of this idea must imply that the architecture of the present contains evidence of inherited characteristics. There seems to be a historical as well as a Darwinian model for this process—the *topos* of *unconscious absorption*, of which the medieval world, with its assimilation and transformation of Roman forms, has stood, ever since the romantic movement, as the prime example.

But there is something strained about thinking of modernism in this way. The main point about modernism, in art as in architecture, was that it stood for a change in the relationship between the present and the past, rather than being the continuation of an existing relationship. No doubt this "epistemological break" could be "explained" by changes in the sociology, technology, and economics of architecture, thus lending "newness" the appearance of being the result of historical causality. But such an explanation is not so easily applied to art in general, and the influence of general artistic theory on modern architecture was as strong, if not stronger, than that of technology, as Giedion so eloquently demonstrated in *Space, Time and Architecture*. It seems, in fact, that the notion of "modernity" in the classical avant-garde can only partially be explained by historicism. For it to be fully comprehended other tendencies have to be taken into account—above all ideas current at the end of the nineteenth century that were strongly antihistoricist, such as can be found in certain writings of Nietzsche on the one hand and in the neo-Kantian formalists on the other, which either deny the logic of historical change or which explain artistic and symbolic forms in terms other than historical.

If we accept such an interpretation of "the modern," the changes in the climate of opinion in the last twenty years must seem as a mere continuation of the "crisis" that struck architecture around 1910—the moment when an apparently irreversible break with history occurred. Even if we were to maintain that the "objective" conditions were never clearly enough determined to justify the break with history demanded by modernist theory, we have to admit that once these theories were in place and had gathered momentum, a wholly new objective cultural situation was created. It is within the context of this new situation that the various reactions against modernism (including the most recent "postmodern" reaction) arose and from which they take their color. Thus all the ways in which postmodernism has attempted to reintroduce historical forms have themselves been unmistakably "modern." They belong more to the modernism they want to supersede than to the tradition they try to invoke. For this reason it would be better to interpret the word *postmodern* to mean not only the revival of historical forms, but all those tendencies, apparently within modernism itself, that have modified its original content.

For, if the present situation is inescapably modern, it also contains aspects alien to the original aspirations of the modern movement. At the level of architectural production, contemporary methods of construction and the design techniques that have grown up around them have continued to develop more or less as predicted by the avant-garde of the 1920s. In this prognosis the theorists of modernism were merely showing intelligent foresight. But they were not equally right in their assumptions of absolutely even development, either on a technical or a cultural level. They assimilated to empirical "scientific" processes all the aesthetic and symbolic absolutes they had inherited from the past and saw these processes as creating a global *Gesamtkunstwerk*. The reality of the present is very different. Two examples of this reality may be cited. One is the modern office block, which, as a function-type, has taken on a far greater importance than was anticipated by modernist theory. Modern corporate buildings, though using the most advanced technology, are not uniform nor rationally segregated as modernist theory would have had them; instead, they compete with one another linguistically within the existing city matrix. At the same time their megastructural dimensions make impossible the control of scale and proportions that avant-garde architects from Sullivan to Mies and Le Corbusier tried to give them.

The second example lies in the discontinuous nature of modern development, and its variety of linguistic forms. This variety is not random; it follows a certain demarcation of function-types, so that separate linguistic codes operate for different types such as office buildings, housing, and museums, and for development within cities and in the suburbs.

Bracing as the freedom resulting from such a pluralistic situation may sometimes be, it cannot in itself sustain a coherent architectural discourse, and it becomes increasingly difficult to measure particular developments against a common standard of architectural values. An essential precondition of the unraveling of this problem would be to clarify the situation that existed when modernist theory was formulated and to see in what way this theory differed from the discourse inherited from the past. "Modern architecture" was characterized by the new relationship that obtained between architecture as art and architecture as the practical provision of shelter. Historically these two aspects of architecture were never wholly separate. The symbolic was a transfiguration of the real (architecture as the intellectual transformation and representation of structure). The artistic component of building was closely bound up with transcendental meaning, and was the architectural equivalent of naturalism in painting. According to the classical theory of naturalism, art penetrated below the surface of the given to show forth the "idea." It was in this sense that architecture could be thought of as the imitation of nature.

But with modernism, art cut itself adrift from what it took to be an extrinsic reality and became an exploration of pure forms, the meanings of which were immanent and reflexive. It was in this guise that art became a paradigm for architecture in the 1920s. The old liaison between architecture as shelter and architecture as transcendental meaning was lost, and a new unity was envisaged within the theory of functionalism, which attributed transcendental value to function itself. This fiction depended on a certain constellation of cultural events; once this constellation was dissolved, the fusion between material purpose and transcendental meaning was also lost. The result is that everything that cannot be attributed to practical convenience is left without a body of theory to support it.

It has been argued that any transcendental theory is unnecessary and, indeed, impossible in the present situation of late capitalism; the disappearance of the master narratives that presided over nineteenth-century historicism and the birth of modernism signals, it is said, the final disappearance of any possibility of, or need for, a general grounding of value. Yet all theories of "decon-struction" that purport to show that philosophy is dead are presented within the format of philosophy itself; they do not accept passively the relativism that they appear to be celebrating.

It is this apparent paradox that leads both to the provisional acceptance of contemporary pluralism in architecture and to a deep concern over the absence of any coherent discourse. These essays are offered as a contribution toward the development of such a discourse.

Acknowledgments

Thanks are due to friends and colleagues who have helped to give substance and clarity to many of the ideas touched on in this book—especially to Mary McLeod, Tony Vidler, and Demetri Porphyrios. Thanks are also due to Mark Rakatansky and Debbi Edelstein for their editorial responsiveness and forbear-ance, and to Cymbre Raub for her help in selecting and processing the illustrations.

Modernity and the Classical Tradition
Architectural Essays 1980–1987

I   Historicism and the
Burden of the Classical

Three Kinds of Historicism

The title of this essay is simply the starting point for an attempt to clarify the confusion that surrounds the word *historicism* in modern architectural criticism, and through this to throw some light on the present situation in architecture, in which a new consciousness of history has replaced the antihistorical bias of the modern movement.

Dictionary definitions (and general usage) suggest that there are three interpretations of *historicism:* (1) the theory that all sociocultural phenomena are historically determined and that all truths are relative; (2) a concern for the institutions and traditions of the past; (3) the use of historical forms. The word *historicism* therefore can be applied to three quite separate objects: the first is a theory of history; the second, an attitude; the third, an artistic practice. There is no guarantee that the three have anything in common. I will investigate them to see how, if at all, they *are* related and then to see what light they throw on the phenomenon sometimes referred to as the *neo-avant-garde.*

The idea that values change and develop with historical time is by now so ingrained in common wisdom that it is difficult to imagine a different point of view. Yet the idea is, historically speaking, of fairly recent origin. It began to take shape in Europe as a whole in the seventeenth century, but was not given a consistent philosophical or historiographic formulation until the rise of the romantic movement in Germany in the late eighteenth century. The word *his-*

Originally published in *Architectural Design* 53, 9/10 (1983).

toricism, as it applies to our first definition, comes from the German word *historismus*. It used to be translated as *historism*, but, probably under the influence of Benedetto Croce, was changed to *historicism*—from the Italian *storicismo*—in the early years of this century.

In the German movement, historicism was connected with idealism and neoplatonism. But the "Idea" had connotations different from those associated with the classical thought of the seventeenth and eighteenth centuries. According to classical thought, cultural values derived from natural law. Indeed, the value of history for historians like Hume and Montesquieu was that it provided evidence of the existence of this natural law. It was necessary, when studying history, to strip away the inessential and accidental and to expose the essential and universal. Through the study of history one learned with David Hume that "human nature was always and everywhere the same." It followed from this that what was of value in the cultural products of this human nature—art and architecture, for example—was equally fixed. Architecture, no less than painting, was an imitation of Nature through the intuition of her underlying laws. History, as the story of the contingent, merely had the effect of obscuring these laws. It is true that the rise of empirical science in the seventeenth century led certain theorists to question the immutable laws of architecture enshrined in the writing of Vitruvius (for instance, Claude Perrault went so far as to say that the rules of proportion and the orders owed their authority to custom), but this was not a universally held view. The majority of architects and theorists of the seventeenth and eighteenth centuries still held the view that good architecture obeyed immutable natural laws. Even Laugier, writing at a time when the notion of taste had already undermined the classical certainties, claimed that Perrault was prompted by the spirit of contrariness and that the rules of architecture could be deduced from a few self-evident axioms based on our observation of nature. The best architecture was that which was close to nature, and that which was closest to nature could be found in the building of the ancients—though sometimes even they had been mistaken, in which case archaeology had to be supplemented with reason.

The idealism of the neoclassical view of architecture was therefore absolutist and depended on a combination of authority, natural law, and reason. Although in many ways the doctrines of neoclassicism differed from those of the Renaissance, the two held that the values of architecture referred to fixed laws, exemplified in Greco-Roman buildings.

The historicist view disputed the epistemology on which this view of architecture depended and gave an entirely different interpretation of the Ideal. According to historicism, the classical conception of a fixed and immutable ideal was, in fact, a false realism; and it tried to apply to the works of man the same objective standards that it applied to the natural world as a whole. But man belonged to a different category from that of inorganic or organic nature. Man and his institutions could be studied only in relation to the context of their historical development. The individual and the social institutions he constructed were governed by a vital, genetic principle, not by fixed and eternal laws. Human reason was not a faithful reflection of abstract truths; it was the rationalization of social customs and institutions, which had evolved slowly and which varied from place to place and from one time to another. The ideal was therefore an aim that emerged from historical experience and contingency. Although it might have been necessary to postulate an ideal that would be ultimately the same for all cultures, it could not be rationally grasped. We could give it only the names that belonged to the values of a local culture at its particular stage of development. Every culture therefore contained a mixture of truth and falsehood when measured against the ideal; equally, each culture could adhere only to its own notion of the true and the false, through values that were immanent in particular social and institutional forms.

In this view, society and its institutions were analogous to the individual. The individual can be defined only in terms unique to himself. Though he may be motivated by what he and his society see as objective norms of belief and conduct, his own essence cannot be reduced to these norms; it is constituted by the contingent factors of his birth and is subject to a unique development. The value of his life cannot be defined in a way that excludes his individuality. It is the same with societies, cultures, and states: they develop according to organic laws which they have internalized in their structures. In them, truth cannot be separated from destiny.

Based on a new notion of history, this view found its chief expression in the field of historiography. The aim of the historian became to research into the past of a particular society for its own sake, not in order to confirm *a priori* principles and provide exemplars, as had been the case with the English and French historians of the eighteenth century. This new project was undertaken in the German-speaking countries in reaction against the French rationalism that had dominated European thought for two centuries, and it coincided with the rise of German national consciousness. In the work of Leopold von Ranke, the first great historian of this school, the writing of history is characterized by two equally important tendencies: the objective and exhaustive examination of facts, and the attempt to penetrate the essential spirit of the country or period being studied. The dialectic between these two aims (which one might call the positivist and the idealist) had already been stated clearly by Wilhelm von Humboldt in his famous essay "On the Historian's Task" of 1821. According to von Humboldt, the events of history are given purpose and structure by a hidden spirit or idea, just as the idea or form is hidden in the infinitely variable forms of the visible world. It is the historian's task to reveal the idea beneath the empirical surface of historical events, just as it is the artist's task to reveal the ideal beneath the accidental appearance of bodies. At the same time, the idea can become apparent only through the detailed study of these events. Any imposition on history of an *a priori* purpose will inevitably distort reality, and it is this *reality* that is the object of historical study.

An ideal that emerges from particular historical events entails a relativizing of cultures, since aspects of the ideal to be revealed will differ from case to case; and this relativizing of the historical view is obviously connected in some way with eclecticism in the practice of art and architecture. Yet eclecticism did not, in itself, result necessarily in a doctrine of relativism. It was the product of an interest in history which developed in the early eighteenth century—a phenomenon of the history of taste before it became connected with German historical theory. Indeed, *returning* to an architecture based on nature—a notion so foreign to the spirit of historicism—was itself one of the products of this new interest in, and attitude toward, history.

The attitude toward history in the eighteenth century was, in fundamental ways, different from that of the Renaissance. The Renaissance had a strong faith in its contemporary world. In returning to classical modes, it picked up the threads of a world that was more modern than recent medieval culture. In the eighteenth century the return to classicism was always accompanied by elements of poetic reverie, nostalgia, and a sense of irretrievable loss. Within the context of this type of historical consciousness, eclecticism took two forms which at first might seem incompatible. On the one hand, different styles could exist side by side, as when one finds a classical temple next to a Gothic ruin at Stowe. On the other hand, one style could come to stand for a dominant moral idea and be connected with an idea of social reform. This happens, for example, in the second half of the eighteenth century in France, when the desire to reform society initiates a return to austere classical forms, such as one finds in the architecture of Ledoux or the paintings of David. What is common to both forms of eclecticism is a strong feeling for the past, an awareness of the passage of historical time, and the ability of past styles to suggest certain poetic or moral ideas. The same motif can be the expression of private taste and the symbol of public morality. Robert Rosenblum[1] gives the example of the Doric temple front forming the entrance to a cave, which was a folly in the garden of the banker Claude Bernard Saint-James before it became an emblem of Revolution in a pageant at Lyon some years later.

Eclecticism depends on the power of historical styles to become the emblems of ideas associated with the cultures that produced them. No doubt this rela-

Piranesi, Ruins at Paestum, Temple of Neptune,
1778

The bridge at Stowe

The Temple of Ancient Virtue at Stowe, near
which stood a Gothic ruin

Claude-Nicolas Ledoux, House of a Milliner,
1773–79. From *L'Architecture considereé sous le
rapport de l'art, des moeurs et de la législation*
(1804).

Jacques-Louis David, *Lictors Returning to Brutus
the Bodies of His Sons*, 1789. Collection of the
Louvre.

  Claude-Louis Chatelet, *Le Rocher, Folie Saint-James Neuilly.* Collection of Jacques Lebel.

Claude Couchet le jeune, *Design for a Revolutionary Pageant*, 1790

tionship first made itself felt in the Renaissance, but by the late eighteenth century historical knowledge had vastly extended its range of cultural models. An interest in Gothic architecture and in the architecture of the orient existed alongside the classical tradition, which was itself augmented by the discovery of Greek architecture. The idea of a return to a strict and primitive classicism based on *a priori* principles and natural law was one aspect of a new situation giving rise to the new possibility of choice. Choice implies a standard of taste and a decision as to the correct norm—whether this norm is based on a relative scale or on an absolute standard.

Returning to our definitions, we see that the "concern for the institutions of the past" and the "use of historical forms" belong to a broader category of historical phenomena than the historicist theory that "all sociocultural phenomena are historically determined." It was not until the historicist theory was formulated that the idea of the relativism of culture values became an issue. The theory made it impossible, in principle, to favor one style over another, since each style was organically related to a particular spatiotemporal culture and could not be judged except on its own terms. Yet historicist thought was not able to accept all that its theory implied. The historian Friedrich Meinecke[2] pointed out that there were two ways in which historicism attempted to avoid the implications of relativism: by setting up one period as a paradigm and by what he called the "flight into the future."

Representing a historical period as a paradigm would seem contrary to the principles of historicism and, in doing so, historical thought was clearly reverting to eclectic practice. But there was a difference: eclecticism had never severed completely its connections with the classical tradition. It had merely qualified this tradition with examples from other styles, either using these styles to give variety to classical themes or using them to purify the notion of classicism itself—as in the case of Gothic and Greek architecture. With romanticism and historicism, the break from classicism was complete. The style now set up as paradigmatic was Gothic, since Gothic represented not just a particular set of poetic associations, but a type of "organic" society. Here we see a coincidence between positivism and historicism similar to that which I have noted already in Leopold von Ranke. For instance, in seeking the essence of Gothic architecture, Viollet-le-Duc reduced it to a set of instrumental principles that could provide a dynamic model for contemporary practice.

The other method by which historicism tried to overcome relativism—the flight into the future—depended upon a different set of ideas. One of the essential notions of historicism was, as I have said, the idea of development. Not only were various cultures the result of geographical and temporal displacement, not only were cultures unique and irreducible to a single set of principles, but they

Horace Walpole, Strawberry Hill, Twickenham,
Holbein Room, 1759

Thomas Rickman and Henry Hutchinson,
Hampton Lucy Church, Warwickshire, 1822–26

were also subject to a law of growth and change. The notion of genetic development was essential. Without it, the various guises in which the ideal appeared in history would be entirely random and arbitrary, since there was no longer any absolute ideal against which to measure them. It was necessary to replace the notion of a fixed ideal, to which historical phenomena should conform, with the notion of a *potential* ideal, which historical events were *leading up to*. Carried to its extreme, this view led to the idea of history as a teleological process, in which all historical events were determined by final causes. History was now oriented toward an apocalyptic future and no longer toward a normative past. It was the philosophers of historicism, particularly Hegel, who stressed in this way the determinism of history, not the historians themselves. Indeed, von Ranke (following von Humboldt) warned against the tendency of philosophy to schematize history by resorting to final causes. To him this was just as unacceptable as the classical notion of natural law because it denied what to the historians was the basis of historical development—the spiritual independence of the historical subject and the operation of free will in history.

Hegelian idealism, with its emphasis on historical teleology, replaced the will of the historical subject with the suprapersonal will of history itself. The ideal was not seen as informing the individual protagonists of history, as von Humboldt and von Ranke taught; it constituted an implacable historical will, of which the historical subject was the unconscious agent.

The Hegelian notion of historical determinism, however much it was misunderstood,[3] had a profound influence on the framework of thought characteristic of the artistic avant-garde in the late nineteenth and early twentieth centuries. Art and architecture could fulfill their historical destinies only by turning their backs on tradition. Only by looking toward the future could they be faithful to the spirit of history and give expression in their works to the spirit of the age. In architecture this meant the continual creation of new forms under the impulse of social and technological development, and the symbolic representation of society through these forms. Historians of the modern movement, such as Giedion, Pevsner, and Banham, have tended to emphasize this developmental aspect of the avant-garde.

But this mode of thought was not the only, and perhaps not the most important, ingredient of the twentieth-century avant-garde. Another influence was what Philippe Junod, in his book *Transparence et opacité*,[4] has called "gnosiological idealism," whose principal theoretician was the nineteenth-century philosopher Konrad Fiedler. Growing out of the general atmosphere of historicist tradition, this theory systematically sought to exclude from artistic creation the last traces of the idea of *imitation*. It rejected the notion that the work of art is a mirror in which one sees something else. Hegel himself was the principal victim of this radical idealism, since he held the view that the work of art was a reflection of an idea external to itself. The notion of the "opacity" of the work of art was developed further by the Russian Formalists of the 1920s, and it became an essential component of avant-garde thinking.

At the opposite extreme, there was in modernism the idea of natural law and a return to the basic principles of artistic form, which was close to the primitive neoclassicism of the Enlightenment. The tension between this and historicism is particularly noticeable in the writings and buildings of Le Corbusier.

It is not these two aspects of modernism that its critics have attacked, but rather the idea of historical determinism. They have correctly pointed out that a blind faith in the future has the effect of handing over control of the architectural environment to market forces and their bureaucratic representatives. A movement that started as the symbolic representation of utopia has ended by becoming a tool of everyday economic practice. Critics have also shown (and equally correctly) that the systematic proscription of history as a source of architectural values cannot be sustained once the initial utopian impetus of modernism has been lost.

What these "postmodernist" critics have been unable to establish is a *theory of history* that will give a firm basis for this newfound historical consciousness. Because their attack has been restricted mostly to two aspects of modernism—historical determinism and historical amnesia—all they have been able to propose is the reversal of these two ideas: (1) history is not absolutely determined; (2) the acceptance of tradition, *in some form*, is the condition of architectural meaning. These two propositions, being reactions to other propositions, remain negative, and lack a systematic and legitimate basis of their own.

The fact that history cannot be considered as determined and teleological in any crude sense leaves open to question the relation between the historicity of all cultural production, on the one hand, and the cumulative and normative nature of cultural values, on the other. We can hardly expect to return to a classical interpretation of history in which a universal natural law is an *a priori* against which one measures all cultural phenomena. One of the chief reasons why this would be inconceivable is that today we have a different relation to history from that of the eighteenth century. In the eighteenth century the dominant classes were well read in the classics and were able to interpret their culture in terms of classical culture, using it to provide examples and models for their conduct. We have seen that the notion of universal norms was a product of a lively and concrete sympathy for the historical past. Today, our knowledge of the past has increased vastly, but it is the province of specialists and is equal and opposite to a widespread ignorance and vagueness about history in our culture. The more our knowledge of the past becomes objective, the less the past can be applied to our own time. The use of the past to supply models for the present depends upon the ideological distortion of the past; and the whole effort of modern historiography is to eliminate these distortions. In this sense, modern historiography is the direct descendant of historicism. As such, it is committed to a relativistic view of the past and resists the use of history to provide direct models.

On the other hand, it is equally difficult to imagine a culture that ignores the historical tradition altogether. The flight into the future, which characterized the phase of historicism that directly affected modernism, deliberately tried to instill a forgetfulness of history. In so doing, it brought to light what may be considered two weaknesses in nineteenth-century historicist thought. First, it did not take account of cultural borrowing. In its concern to stress the uniqueness of each culture, it overlooked the extent to which all cultures, even the most "indigenous," are based on the ideas and principles of other, pre-existent cultures. There has never been such a thing as an absolutely pure culture; to demonstrate this, one has only to mention the attraction that various proto-renaissances exerted on the medieval world and the influence that the classical world never ceased to exert on European culture.

The second weakness of historicism (closely related to the first) is that it tended to suppress the role that the establishment of norms and types has always played in cultural development. It confused two things that are, in fact, unrelated: it confused the way in which cultures might be studied with the way in which cultures operate. While it might be fruitful to study history as if the culture under examination were a unique organism, it does not follow that it was such an organism in fact. How, for instance, could a historicist study a culture that believed in natural law, and in the principle of the imitation of the idea, without somehow contradicting his own method? To do this, historical analysis would have to reconcile two contradictory principles within itself. Paradoxical as this may seem, this is an important principle that must be faced. It suggests that our culture—and our architecture, as one of its manifestations— must make the same reconciliation. The uniqueness of our culture, which is the product of historical development, must be reconciled with the palpable fact that it operates within a historical context and contains within itself its own historical memory.

In what way can cultural memory manifest itself in architecture today? In my opinion it cannot do this by reverting to eclecticism, if by eclecticism we mean something belonging to eighteenth- and nineteenth-century culture. I have tried to show that in the eighteenth and nineteenth centuries eclecticism depended on the power of architectural style to become a sign or emblem for a certain set of ideas. But this depended on a knowledge of, and sympathetic identification with, the styles of the past and an ability to subject those styles to ideological distortions—distortions that were nonetheless predicated on a thorough knowledge of the styles themselves. Architecture is a form of knowledge by experience. But it is precisely this element of inward knowledge and experience that is lacking today. When we try to recover the past in architecture, we cross a chasm—the chasm of the late nineteenth and early twentieth centuries, during which the power of architectural style to convey definite meanings disappeared entirely. Modern eclecticism is no longer ideologically active, as it was in the nineteenth century. When we revive the past now, we tend to express its most general and trivial connotations; it is merely the "pastness" of the past that is evoked. The phenomenon was already recognized eighty years ago by Aloïs Riegl, who drew attention to the two popular attitudes toward artistic works then prevalent: "newness" and "oldness." As an emblem of "pastness," modern historical recovery actually resists too accurate a memory of past styles; it is only in this way that it can become an item of cultural consumption. As modernism itself was recuperated by capitalism, so is "postmodernism" in all its guises. Modernism and "postmodernism" are two sides of the same coin. They are both essentially "modern" phenomena and are equally remote from the attitude toward history of the eighteenth and nineteenth centuries.

Given the fact that what we produce today is bound to be specifically modern, no matter how we incorporate the past into our work, we should look at that other tradition—the tradition of modernism—to see which of its elements inevitably persist in our attitude toward works of art and architecture. I have mentioned two aspects that are independent of the notion of historical determinism and the flight into the future: the opacity of the work of art and the search for primitive sources. Opacity denies that the work of art is merely a reflection or imitation of some model, whether this model is thought of as a platonic form or as consisting of the "real" world. In this sense it resists both realist idealism and naturalism. But it is not inconsistent with the idea of historical memory. By giving priority to the autonomy of artistic disciplines, it allows, even demands, the persistence of tradition as something that is internalized in these disciplines. The artistic tradition is one of the "objective facts" that is transformed by the creative act.

It seems to me, therefore, that it is valid to approach the problem of tradition in architecture as the study of architecture as an autonomus discipline—a discipline which incorporates into itself a set of aesthetic norms that is the result of historical and cultural accumulation and which takes its meaning from this. But these aesthetic values can no longer be seen as constituting a closed system of rules or as representing a fixed and universal natural law. The notions of the opacity of the work of art and the search for basic principles do not presuppose that architecture is a closed system which has no contact with outside life, with the nonaesthetic. The aesthetic comes into being anew through the existence of a particular material situation, even if it is not wholly conditioned by this situation. Today's historians tend toward investigation of material conditions of the artistic production of the past; today's architects should be equally aware of the transformation of the tradition brought about by these conditions.

What I have said implies that historicism, considered as the theory by which all sociocultural phenomena are historically determined, must still form the basis of our attitude toward history. But the sleight of hand by which historicist idealism replaced the fixed ideal with an emergent idea can no longer be accepted. Such a unitary and mystical concept is bound to lead to systems of thought—both political and artistic—that presuppose what, in fact, remains to be proved: that any given historical system is an organic unity leading inevitably to the progress of mankind.

On the contrary, all systems of thought, all ideological constructs, are in need of constant, conscious criticism; and the process of revision can come about only on the assumption that there is a higher and more universal standard against which to measure the existing system. History provides both the ideas that are in need of criticism and the material out of which this criticism is forged. An architecture that is constantly aware of its own history, but constantly critical of the seductions of history, is what we should aim for today.

Notes

1 Robert Rosenblum, *Transformations in Late Eighteenth Century Art* (Princeton: Princeton University Press, 1967), p. 127.

2 Friedrich Meinecke, "Geschichte und Gegenwort" (History in relation to the present), 1933, in *Vom Geschichtlichen Sinn und vom Sinn der Geschichte*, 2nd edition (1939), pp. 14ff; cited by Karl Hinrichs in Friedrich Meinecke, *Historism: The Rise of a New Historical Outlook*, trans. J. E. Anderson (London: Routledge and Kegan Paul, 1972), p. li.

3 In the *Introduction to the Philosophy of World History*, Hegel lays greater stress on the need for an empirical approach than is often supposed.

4 Philippe Junod, *Transparence et opacité* (Lausanne: L'Age d'homme, 1976).

Vernacular Classicism

The theories of architecture put forward in a given period often consist of transformations and recombinations of earlier theories. Moreover, it sometimes happens that a later theory reverses an earlier one and that two concepts previously antithetical may become allies.

The phrase "vernacular classicism" seems to be an example of this type of transformation. To all appearances it is an oxymoron. Throughout the self-consciously classical periods—both Hellenistic and post-Renaissance—*classic* stands to *vernacular* as high art stands to low art, though the actual words were not used until after the romantic movement. In romanticism, ideas associated with the vernacular were given a value independent of the place they had held in the classical hierarchy of artistic styles. The "low mimetic" style became the model for art in general and was used to express the kinds of serious ideas previously reserved for the "high mimetic" style.[1] But in romantic thought, the meanings carried by the two terms remained antithetical.

The word *classical* or *classic* was not used generally in connection with architecture or the visual arts until after the German romantic movement, when the opposition classic/romantic was first coined.[2] Previously, when critics or historians wished to refer to the art of Greece or Rome, they usually spoke of the "antique." Nonetheless, in poetics the word *classical* was used as early as the second century AD, when the grammarian Aulus Gellius used it to distinguish between the *scriptor classicus* and the *scriptor proletarius*. The words *classicus* and

Originally published in *Architectural Design* 54, 5/6 (1984).

proletarius were borrowed from Roman tax law; *classicus* referred to the first of the four social orders supposedly founded by Servius Tullius. In this metaphorical translation to literature, the *scriptor classicus* was he who wrote for the few, and the *scriptor proletarius* for the many.

The word *classicus* was revived in the Renaissance, first in Italy, then in France and England, when it meant either texts used for instruction in schools or standard Greek and Roman texts worthy of imitation by modern authors. In this context, *classical* had the connotation of "highest class," and it entailed the stylistic transformation of the various vernaculars of post-medieval Europe in conformity with Greek or Roman models. It need hardly be said that this is one of the senses in which the word is still used today, though its normative implications are no longer taken for granted.[3]

It seems quite legitimate to use *classical* in this sense to describe the architecture of antiquity as well as the literature. The connection was indeed made in the Renaissance and in the following three centuries during which classical theory dominated all aspects of European culture. The post-Renaissance period revived not only many of the artistic practices of the ancients, but also their artistic theory: that of Vitruvius in architecture and those of Aristotle's *Poetics* and Horace's *Art of Poetry* in literature and painting. It is chiefly from these sources that academic classicism derived such fundamental ideas as *imitation* and *decorum*.

Thus, both in a certain phase of antiquity itself and in the Renaissance, *classical* signified practices codified in a system of canonic rules which claimed superiority over all other practices, whether these were taken as "grammatical" in a narrow sense, or more broadly "artistic." A similar process had taken place in India in about the fourth century BC, when the ancient language of the Vedas was codified by the grammarians and was called Sanskrit (from the roots *san*, together, and *Kr*, make).

The word *vernacular* is equally derived from social and economic concepts. *Verna* meant slave, and *vernacular* signified a person residing in the house of his master. Hence the later applied meaning—first to language and then to the arts—of local, indigenous, and lowly forms.

Within the context of European history, then, the word *vernacular* can be taken to apply to practices of *making* (linguistic, constructional, etc.) that are either anterior to or untouched by classical theory and practice. Such practices, continuing in parallel with those of "high art," were recognized by classical theory and were placed by it at the lowest level of the artistic hierarchy (in Serlio's representation of Comedy, for example, where the *fabrique* consists of "vernacular" buildings arranged without symmetry, in contrast to the classical symmetry of the noble style more appropriate for Tragedy).

Serlio, *Scena Tragica*. From *The Five Books of Architecture* (1611).

Serlio, *Scena Comica*. From *The Five Books of
Architecture* (1611).

After the breakup of the classical system at the end of the eighteenth century, however, these nonclassical vernacular forms of art began to be studied in and for themselves. They began to be thought of not as "styles" within a larger system, but as forms of art possessing their own significance, challenging the universalist claims of the classical canon. Art and literary criticism, after the onset of romanticism and historicism, attempted to reverse the values of the classical and the nonclassical (e.g., to establish medieval art as superior to classical art) or to relativize all systems according to some theory of historical development.

Eric Auerbach's seminal literary study *Mimesis* (1946) is an outstanding example of the latter tradition. Auerbach distinguished between the typology of classical literature and that of various nonclassical texts, notably the Bible and medieval literature. Whereas, according to Auerbach, classical literature was characterized by "an abundant display of connectives . . . a precise gradation of temporal, comparative and concessive hypotaxes . . . and participle construction," the Bible and the writings of the medieval period had a tendency to "string different pictures together like beads" and to "divide the course of events into a mosaic of parcelled pictures."[4] He saw these and other related features as belonging to a specifically Christian tradition whose ideas could not have been expressed in terms of classical decorum, since they demanded a mixture of styles: the treating of noble subjects in an ignoble setting.

Whether or not it would be legitimate to identify this kind of paratactic literary structure with "vernacular" art in general, it seems evident that Auerbach is describing a general nonclassical tradition which flourished in the early period of Christian culture and which owed a great deal to local traditions. Clearly there are problems in trying to apply this paradigm to *all* medieval art. The Gothic cathedral, for instance, is by no means a "vernacular" building. It is a codified representational system, and, as Panofsky showed, was organized with a logic that was analogous to scholastic thought. It can therefore be claimed that High Gothic art had many of the underlying characteristics of classicism. Indeed it was itself based on antique architecture, in the form in which it had survived the Dark Ages and as modified by northern vernacular habits. But medieval "imitation" of building allows for a greater degree of paratactic freedom than is permitted in the predominantly hypotactic structures of classical architecture. The acceptance of the unequal towers of Chartres and other cathedrals and the additive and pragmatic arrangement of monastic complexes are cases in point. In contrast to this, a classical building was conceived as a body whose parts, perfectly distinct in themselves, were related to each other in a coordinated and self-sufficient hierarchy, on the analogy of the human body. The concept of "order" which this exemplifies, and which characterized classical thought, was

Leon Battista Alberti, San Andrea in Mantua,
designed 1470

Strasbourg Cathedral

summed up in the Pythagorean epigram "order and measure (*taxis* and *symmetria*) are pleasing, disorder and excess (*ataxis* and *asymmetria*) are ugly and baneful."[5] Whatever logic the Gothic cathedral may have possessed, it did not represent this kind of order. It may have been intended to lead the faithful to a vision of perfection, but it did not in itself constitute a bodily image of such perfection.

What appealed to the romantics about medieval art was its mixture of styles and its parataxis. As evidence of a liking for a mixture of styles we can quote Ruskin in *The Stones of Venice*. "Everything in nature," he says, "has good and evil in it, and artists, considered as searchers after truth are . . . to be divided into three great classes. . . . Those on the right perceive and pursue the good and leave the evil; those in the centre, *the greatest*, perceive and pursue the good and the evil together and the whole thing verily as it is; those on the left perceive and pursue the evil and leave the good" (my italics).[6] Ruskin's "three great classes" are, of course, the same as those mentioned by Aristotle in the *Poetics*; he simply inverts them. As for the romantics' love of parataxis, we find it in both literary and architectural criticism. In one of his "Fragments," Novalis describes the ideal modern poetry thus: "Disconnected, incoherent narratives that nonetheless have associations, like *dreams*. Simply poems that are perfectly harmonious, but also without coherence or any meaning . . . which must be like pure fragments of the most disparate ideas."[7] A similar attraction for the irrational and incomprehensible is found in the young Goethe's remarks about Strasbourg Cathedral: "With what unlooked for emotions did the sight surprise me . . . a sensation of wholeness, greatness filled my soul, which, composed of a thousand harmonious details, I could savour and enjoy, yet by no means understand or explain."[8] Friedrich Schlegel's descriptions of Gothic are couched in similar terms.

The notion of parataxis, or "laying things side by side" might seem, at first sight, incompatible with that other crucial concept of romantic aesthetics: organic wholeness. But for the romantics the fragmentary and apparently disordered surface of a work of art, far from indicating a lack of organic unity, was in fact a sign of a more profound unity, which escaped analysis because it sprang from the depths of the artist's unconscious mind.

The "primitivism" we find in the Enlightenment is very different from this romantic approach to vernacular architecture. The "return" is not to a particular, idiosyncratic culture, based on local craft traditions; it is to the sources of architecture as a universal language obeying the necessities of natural law.

Neoclassicism looked back to a "natural" architecture that must have existed before society became corrupted, or before architecture became fragmented into all those "dialects" that historical research and travel had uncovered. The pos-

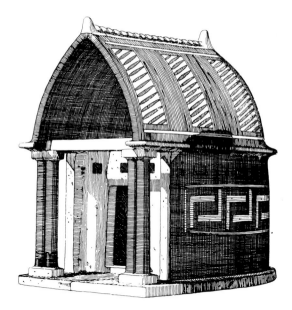

Temple or house from Perachora, c. 750–725 BC

The Market House, Tetbury, c. 1700

tulation of a common, primitive culture, which Laugier shares to some extent with Rousseau, does not involve the empirical discovery of an actual vernacular; it is an hypothesis based on what logically should have been the case, conflating the logical with the chronological.

We do not know a great deal about the pre-monumental architecture of ancient Greece, but what we do know leads us to believe that it had no relation to Laugier's primitive hut. Nor is it certain what the sources of Greek monumental architecture were.[9] Laugier was no more concerned with the "real" Mediterranean vernacular than was Rousseau with a historical primitive society. He was concerned with a distillation of classical doctrine. He was not seeking to return to the earliest hours of man, but to the pure sources of classical architecture. This process entailed, not the discovery of vernacular building, but the *revernacularization* of classicism with which to substantiate a myth of origins.

Therefore, when we define *vernacular* in terms of the eighteenth-century notion of the primitive, we are involved in an argument that is characteristically classical. The myth of origins, as recorded by Vitruvius, was an integral part of classical doctrine and was necessary to the establishment of classicism as a universal system based on nature. But to "understand" a particular belief in historical terms is not necessarily to subscribe to it. Today we can hardly fail to see the attempt of the eighteenth century to create an architectural ontology as having been bounded by eighteenth-century epistemology. The belief in the essential being of architecture, and of its origins, is consistent with, and inextricable from, the ideas of the eighteenth-century grammarians. Like language, architecture was held to be a universal form of knowledge, but one that was not thoroughly worked out. It had come about through the rough-and-ready ordering of our representations. The history and practice of both language and architecture presented the observer with the elements of truth; it was up to him to unravel the skein that had been wound up through the centuries without system, and to put its threads into the right order.[10] It is only in terms of such a linguistics that we can understand what the eighteenth century meant by ontological truth, and how it was applied in architectural discourse.

When, therefore, we use the expression "vernacular classicism," we are describing a process by which classicism, within the terms of its own theory of language, recreates its own origins. It is a movement backward within a closed *episteme*. In all attempts to discover an ontology of architecture within classicism (just as in all those cases where the classical system filtered down to local builders—from Italian farms to English market halls), we are likely to find traces of those elements of high style which originally belonged to a sophisticated and highly developed architecture of monuments—the very antithesis of vernacular building.

Notes

1 For a definition of high and low mimetic styles, see Northrop Frye, *Anatomy of Criticism* (Princeton: Princeton University Press, 1971).

2 By Friedrich Schlegel; see Rene Wellek, *History of Modern Criticism* (Cambridge: Cambridge University Press, 1981), vol. 2, p. 14.

3 Vestiges of the normative status of classical studies are curiously preserved in the Latin textbooks still used in schools in England. In them one still finds the general rules of grammar set out in the opening pages, as if the study of grammar and the study of Latin were one and the same thing.

This example shows how the way of thinking engendered by classical texts (for example, in terms of the grammatical rules of language) has remained attached to the circumstances of its origin, and has superimposed itself on an indigenous and more empirical tradition. One learns grammar in connection with Latin, not in connection with one's own language, which is thought of as being "without rules."

4 Eric Auerbach, *Mimesis* (Princeton: Princeton University Press, 1968), ch. 5, "Roland against Ganelon," and ch. 7, "Adam and Eve."

5 Timpanaro-Cardini, *Pitagorici, Testimonianze e Frammenti* (Florence, 1958), p. 299; quoted in David Summers, *Michelangelo and the Language of Art* (Princeton: Princeton University Press, 1981), p. 314.

6 John Ruskin, *The Stones of Venice* (London: George Allen, 1886), vol. 2, ch. 6, "The nature of Gothic," p. 187.

7 Novalis, *Oeuvres complètes*, ed. A. Guerue (Paris, 1975); quoted in Tzvetan Todorov, *Theories of the Symbol* (Ithaca: Cornell University Press, 1982), p. 176.

8 Wolfgang Von Goethe, "Von deutscher Baukunst" (1772), English translation in *Goethe on Art*, ed. John Gage (London: Scolar Press, 1980), pp. 103–12.

9 Cf. J. J. Coulton, *Greek Architects at Work* (London: Granada, 1982), ch. 3, "The Problem of Beginning."

10 Cf. Michel Foucault, *The Order of Things* (New York: Pantheon, 1970), ch. 4, "Speaking."

Composition versus the Project

In the Anglo-Saxon countries the ideological conflict symbolized by the opposition *composizione/projettazione* is marked less by a word that acts as the antonym of *composition* than by the simple exclusion of the word from the critical vocabulary. In the postwar years, this proscription was typical of an architectural climate that was moral, utilitarian, and pragmatic. Criticism in this period ignored the ambiguity of the relationship between the idea of composition and the artistic avant-gardes. This essay will address some of these ambiguities.

Perhaps the most familiar use of the word *composition* is in the context of music, where in the nineteenth century the word must have had progressive rather than retrogressive connotations. This development was theoretically grounded in neo-Kantian aesthetics and German formalism, in which, as a kind of extension of Lessing, painting, music, and the arts in general were to be studied empirically under the two headings of material means and psychological reception. Paradoxically, these investigations into the means and effects special to each of the arts led to music becoming the paradigm of all the arts. One possible reason for this was that in the nineteenth-century campaign against traditional theories of imitation—or at least against the increasingly realistic interpretation of these theories—music was seen as the art least contaminated by an object of imitation. *Composition* came to mean a creative procedure in which the artist created "out of nothing" and arranged his material according to laws generated

Originally published in *Casabella* 50 (January/February 1986): 11–18.

within the work itself. At the same time the example of music made it possible to rethink the relationships between form and content characteristic of classical theory. Form was no longer thought of as a means of expressing a certain idea, but as indissoluble from, and coextensive with, the idea. *Composition* therefore was able to stand for an aesthetic of immanence in which art became an independent kind of knowledge of the world and was no longer, as it had been both in the medieval and the classical traditions, the means by which certain "truths" or concepts were given rhetorical clothing.[1]

The extent to which this general formalist tradition entered into the theory and practice of the twentieth-century architectural avant-garde was obscured by the doctrine of functionalism, which had the effect of reactivating an apparently more traditional and *retardataire* view of the "content" of the work of architecture, in the guise of the "architectural program."

If, however, we exclude certain extreme "functionalists," we have to admit that formalism was one of the strongest impulses behind architectural modernism.[2] But the relationship between architecture and formalism was somewhat different from that which existed in the other arts. More than they, architecture maintained a stubborn stylistic eclecticism throughout the nineteenth century. This seems to be due to the fact that in architecture reference to the tradition is by means of syntagmata, figures, or tropes of such relative size that they refuse to be reabsorbed into the texture of the work as a whole. In the other arts it was possible throughout the nineteenth century to maintain a connection with tradition while at the same time breaking with many traditional procedures. (One thinks for example of the loss of tonal centrality in the work of Robert Schumann). What was left of the tradition was subtle enough not immediately to give the impression that it was a quotation or imitation of previous forms. In this sense architecture seems the most archaic of the arts. Until the Renaissance it was common in all the arts for new work to reiterate extensive passages of old work without any suggestion of what we would now call plagiarism. Architecture is the only art where this still holds.

At least in part, the purpose of functionalism was to try to exorcise those persistent forms whose semantic and expressive functions depended on the repetition of previous forms. To this extent, functionalism was an alibi for a system of forms that were to be innocent of stylistic contamination. The "meaning" of a building could now be transferred from its form to its content, cutting form adrift and leaving it free to develop its own immanent meanings.

This process depended on compositional procedures precisely to the extent that the architecture avoided the repetition of previous formal solutions and the meanings embedded in them. This is evident if we take the example of neoplasticism. Though Mondrian was a painter, he worked closely with architects, with whom he shared a certain body of doctrine. His writings contain a litany of terms like "dynamic equilibrium," "mutual relations," "balance," "movement," "constructive elements," "relations of position," "determinate and objective composition," all of which are part of an attempt to develop a vocabulary with which to describe formal relationships in space. Moholy-Nagy was another theorist who developed a compositional terminology. The following quotation from his *Von Material zu Architektur* not only demonstrates this, but also shows the connection between functionalism and formalism already mentioned.

The elements necessary to the fulfillment of a function of a building unite in a spatial creation that can become a spatial experience for us. The ordering of space in this case is not more than the most economical union of planning methods and human needs. The current program plays an important role in this but does not entirely determine the type of space created.[3]

It is clear that function—determining relationships that *can* become a spatial (that is, formal) experience but that does not *entirely* determine the type of space (form) created—is merely a mask for form (space). All the escape hatches are carefully left open to provide a retreat from too rigorous an interpretation of functional determinism.

Function, in this system of ideas, provides a rationale for compositional play. It also acts as a catalyst. The main difference between modernist and classical composition is that in the former there is a high degree of freedom in the relationships between the parts. It is not so much that the elements themselves are infinite. Moholy-Nagy's definition of space as "the relationship between the positions of bodies"[4] suggests that, for him at least, the elements were given and finite ("found"). It was their possibilities of combination that were infinite, since the rules for these were topological (they were "kinds of" relationships). The rest was up to the free invention of the architect.

When we turn from theory to practice we find the same thing. Rietveld's house for Madame Schroeder is a carefully composed three-dimensional object. The play of lines and planes is not the result of constructional necessity, even though the memory of such necessity enters into their semantics. In the numerous projects that usually preceded Le Corbusier's final solutions (for example, The Palace of the Soviets or the Centrosoyus),[5] one can sense the exhilaration with which the architect plays with all the permutations of relationship between the fixed elements. Functional distribution is only one among many types of variable that have to be synthesized into the solution. It is the degree to which these kinds of design are free from fixed rules of combination and are active and dynamic in their free play of forms, not the presence or absence of composition as such, that differentiates them from academic composition.

Piet Mondrian, *Composition with Red, Yellow, and Blue*, 1922

Gerrit Rietveld, Schroeder house, Utrecht, 1924

Le Corbusier, Palais des Soviets, Moscow, preliminary sketch

Nevertheless, despite the obvious importance of composition in modernist practice and despite the fact that the idea of composition carried with it progressivist overtones of artistic formalism, the connotations of the word in avant-garde circles were overwhelmingly negative and were irrevocably connected with the academic tradition and the architecture of stylistic imitation represented by the Ecole des Beaux-Arts. Therefore it might be helpful to glance at the role composition played in this tradition.

For Quatremère de Quincy the word *composition* was associated with the decline in the great building enterprises of the past and the resulting proliferation of vast and unbuildable paper projects. As he remarked in his *Dictionnaire*:

One must say that modern times, and above all the schools, have perhaps allowed too much architectural composition to enter the practical exercises of students. One might observe that this abuse is derived, in its own way, from the same cause that multiplied the discourses and compositions of the rhetoreticians in ancient Rome.[6]

But the word *composition* does not seem to have come into general use in the Ecole des Beaux-Arts until the mid-nineteenth century. Before this the word *disposition* was more common.[7] Its use seems to be connected with a cluster of phenomena, one of the most important of which is eclecticism. Composition becomes a means by which rules of design common to all styles can be established. Already in the case of Dubut and Durand the weakening of meanings carried by the classical figures made it both possible and necessary to reduce these figures to ciphers in a system of combinations. *Composition* in academic usage seems to presuppose a body of rules that are astylar. It is true that before the 1880s the stylistic tradition was never abandoned. But there is much evidence in nineteenth-century architectural criticism that the styles seemed increasingly "inauthentic." The apparent vitality of stylistic eclecticism in the nineteenth century is matched only by the virulence with which it was attacked from all quarters. Within the context of this collapse of "stylistic conviction," both the French and the English depended increasingly on compositional formulae, whether these were more or less regular, as in the Ecole de Beaux-Arts, or irregular and picturesque, as in the English Gothic revival and Free Style.

The idea of composition was directly inherited by the twentieth-century avant-garde from the academic tradition. Moreover, in both cases it derived its authority from the same cause, namely the lack of any culturally imposed rules of style. If this was indeed the case, it would not be the first time that a revolutionary movement borrowed the structures and institutions of the very regime that it sought to destroy.

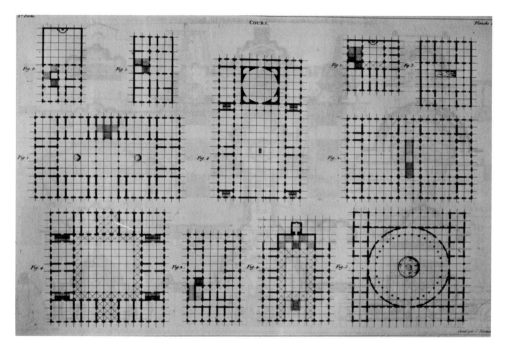

40

J.-N.-L. Durand, comparative table of courtyards. From *Précis des leçons données à l'Ecole
Polytechnique* (1802–5).

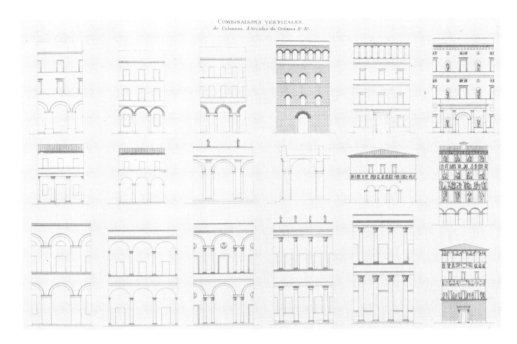

J.-N.-L. Durand, comparative drawings of facades. From *Précis des leçons données à l'Ecole
Polytechnique* (1802–5).

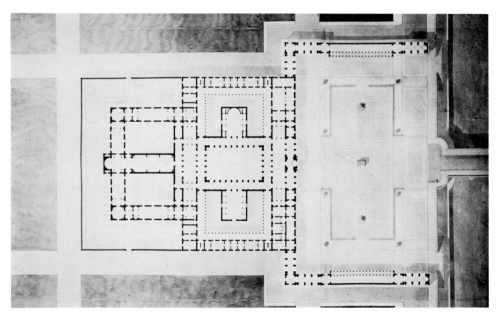

Louis Duc, Hôtel de Ville pour Paris, 1825,
upper floor plan

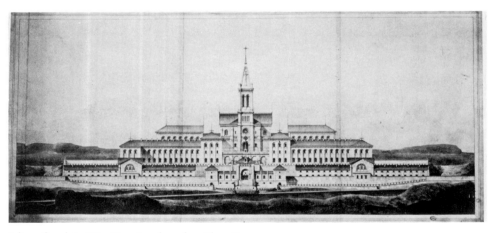

Julien Guadet, "Un Hospice dans les Alpes,"
Premier Grand Prix, 1864, elevation

William Butterfield, Saint Mary's Vicarage, Coal-
pit Heath, 1845

Ludwig Mies van der Rohe, Wolf house, Guben,
1926

Walter Gropius, Masters' house, Dessau (Bauhaus), 1928

44

One of the ways in which composition was assimilated by modernism is illustrated by the wave of books on composition that overtook architectural discourse, at least in the Anglo-Saxon countries, in the first decades of the twentieth century. Probably none of these books is of any great intrinsic value, but they do show how avant-garde ideas and attitudes filtered down to the more conservative ranks of the profession and the role that composition played in this process. An interesting example is provided by two books by the English architect Howard Robertson, *The Principles of Architectural Composition* and *Modern Architectural Design*.[8] The impulse for these books came from the revival of classicism, which was such a general phenomenon in Europe and America in the early twentieth century. (The frequency with which the change from the Gothicizing forms of National Romanticism and Art Nouveau to those of classicism was a prelude to modernism is demonstrated in the work of Peter Behrens, Karl Moser, and Le Corbusier, among others.) The message of Robertson's first book is that there are fundamental rules of composition in architecture that are independent of styles. Styles have relative value: they depend on the revolutions of taste. The values of architecture, on the contrary, are permanent. Robertson studies these under such headings as unity, composition of masses, contrast, proportion in detail, scale, composition of the plan, and relation of plan to elevation. Clearly these categories are based on the teaching of the Ecole des Beaux-Arts, where Robertson had studied. They also depend on classical theory insofar as they claim that the rules of architecture are transhistorical. Most of the examples are of traditional buildings; nevertheless there are certain similarities between the arguments in the book and those in Le Corbusier's *Vers une architecture*.

In his second book Robertson enlarges on some of the themes in the first. The significance of this second volume lies in the fact that most of the examples are "modern," and the tone of the book is cautiously avant-garde. The author wants to show that applying the universal principles of architecture does not preclude a "new architecture" suitable to a new way of life. If there is nothing contradictory in this it is because the "principles" are entirely astylar. Robertson's "new architecture" tends to be rather anodyne, and his argument entirely lacks Le Corbusier's dialectical power. But these two books show clearly the continuing role of composition in the transition from a classicizing to a modernist position.

Given these palpable connections, where should we look for the origins of the violent antagonism of the twentieth-century avant-garde to composition? If one of the sources of the modernism of the 1920s was the classical revival and the belief in the transhistorical values of architecture, another was the romantic movement, with its concern for the processes of generation, growth, and development. It is from this system of ideas that the avant-garde drew its sus-

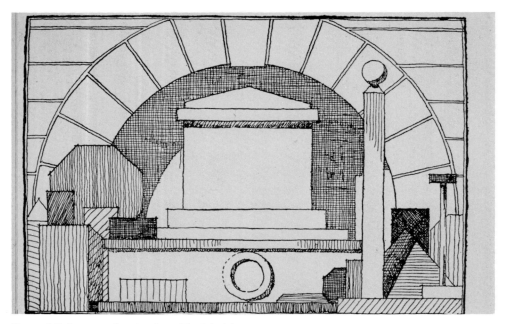

Howard Robertson, drawing from *The Principles
of Architectural Composition* (1924)

46

Folies Bergère building, which Robertson, in
Modern Architectural Design (1932), compares to
the Van Nelle factory in Rotterdam

Brinkmann and Van der Vlugt, Van Nelle factory, Rotterdam, 1926–30, as it appears in Robertson's *Modern Architectural Design*

picion of composition, and the notions of separate parts and forms that came with it.

Such ideas of finality go back far beyond the Ecole des Beaux-Arts; they reverberate through the whole of the classical tradition. *Composition* in its modern sense may be of fairly recent origin, but the set of ideas to which it owes its origin has its roots in antiquity. It concerns the notion of arranging the parts of architecture like elements in a syntax, and according to certain *a priori* rules, to form a whole. This general sense is exemplified in Alberti's artistic theory. In *Della Pittura* Alberti uses the word *composition* to mean "the properties with which the parts of the things seen are presented together in the picture" ("ragione di dipingere con la quale le parti delle cose vedute si porgono insieme in pictura").[9] The equivalent word in *De Re Aedificatoria* is *collatio*—one of three terms within the concept *concinnitas,* the other two being *numerus* and *finito.*[10] Of course, for Alberti the word *collatio* does not mean exactly the same as our word *composition.* Generally speaking, classical theory between the sixteenth and eighteenth centuries was primarily concerned with arranging the parts of an architectural body in a system of proportions. In François Blondel's *Cours, composition* refers to the application of musical proportions to the orders.[11] It is not until the eighteenth century that the problem of arranging or juxtaposing different bodies to form a whole begins to take precedence over the arrangement of parts within a single body. But both these kinds of composition depend equally on the idea of a whole being made out of parts that are, in some sense, already given, so that it is always possible to think of this whole as an aggregation, however much the parts may overlap to give a strong unitary reading.[12]

These ideas persist into the late eighteenth century, and not only in architecture. As Lionel Gossman has pointed out, the model of culture for the eighteenth-century historian was that of "a mechanism of functionally interrelated parts, each of which could in principle be detached and studied on its own." According to this way of thinking, a type of organization (such as chivalry) "could appear in different moments in history, in different guises, as part of similarly structured societies and to fulfill similar needs."[13] Here the idea of *composition* is extended to mean the combination of parts found in different historical or geographical contexts (somewhat recalling the Aristotelian doctrine of "scattered beauties").

This whole manner of thinking about art and about history was rejected by the romantics. It was Novalis who gave one of the most succinct definitions of the aim of romanticism in the mimetic arts: "There is a symptomatic imitation and a genetic imitation. The only living one is the second."[14] As Tzvetan Todorov points out, this implies a shift of attention away from the relationship among forms (which is thought of as the imitation of symptoms and connected

Roland Fréart, "The Corinthian Order." From
Parallèle de l'architecture (1650).

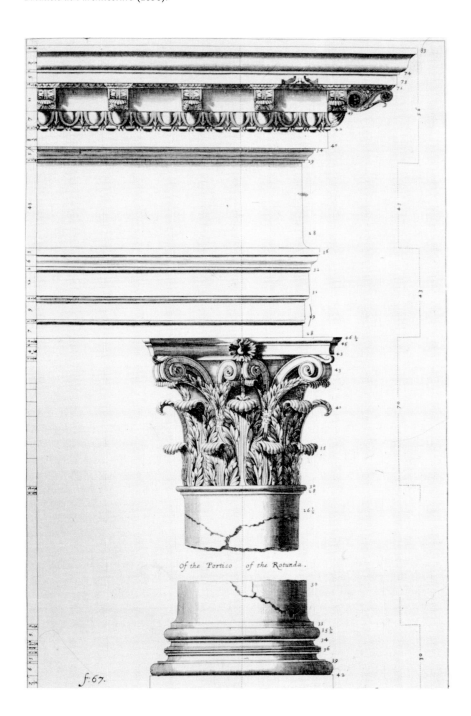

Of the Portico of the Rotunda.

f. 67.

49

Claude-Nicolas Ledoux, Maison de commerce,
perspective. From *L'Architecture consideréé sous le
rapport de l'art, des moeurs et de la législation* (1804)

to composition) to the process of production (genetic imitation).[15] In Schelling we find a similar idea: "works born of juxtaposition of forms . . . would still remain wholly without beauty since what must give the work of art as a whole its beauty can no longer be form but something above form, namely: the essence . . . the expression of the spirit that must dwell there."[16]

In the realm of architecture it was Gothic that most often exemplified these organicist ideas. The kind of eclecticism proposed by Legrand, Hope, and Raoul-Rochette[17]—an eclecticism in which one would select the best parts from all styles and compose them into new wholes—was thought of by the adherents of the Gothic school as entailing "les accouplements monstrueux." The unity of style which Gothicists like Viollet-le-Duc demanded was based on an analogy between architecture and organic nature. Viollet expressed this idea when he said that one should be able to deduce the form of an entire building from the observation of one of its parts. In such a synecdochic structure, it would be absurd to talk about composition. The final forms of architecture, as of nature, should be the result of a certain principle of structuration, from which the form would follow automatically without the intervention of the "composer" artist's conscious judgment. It was no more necessary to imagine the architect "composing" a building than it was to imagine God interfering with the events in the universe after the initial creative act, which would contain the seed of all that followed.

Viollet is normally thought of as a rationalist, and the avant-garde of the 1920s has been seen as lying within this rational heritage in its promotion of an architecture based on the application of industrial production and mechanization. But it is sometimes forgotten that for Viollet-le-Duc, as for Le Corbusier, to name but two of the principal actors in this tradition, there was a strong analogy between mechanical and organic forms. This fusion of apparently contradictory ideas has a long history. M. H. Abrams has pointed out that in early nineteenth-century theory there was often mutual infiltration between mechanistic and organicist beliefs, with mechanists claiming that organisms were higher-order machines and organicists claiming that machines were rudimentary types of organisms.[18]

If, as I suggest, the idea of composition is intimately connected with the conflict between the classical and the romantic traditions, the concept that would best represent the antonym of composition would probably be expressed by the word *system*. In spite of the continued use of composition as a technique of design, there has been a persistent tendency within architectural modernism to gravitate toward a concept of the building as a system. No doubt this tendency ultimately owes a great deal to German transcendental idealism, to the notion that the art and architecture of any period should be a reflection of the Zeitgeist

Eugène-Emmanuel Viollet-le-Duc, diagrammatic section through the aisle of a Gothic cathedral. From *Dictionnaire raisonné de l'architecture française du XI au XVI siècle*, 4 (1875).

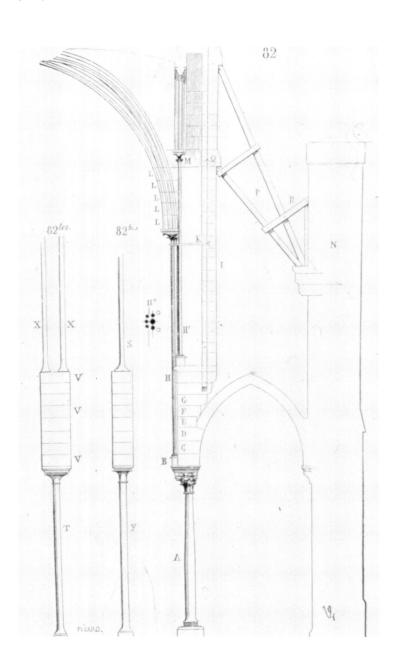

Le Corbusier, Pavillon Suisse, 1930–32, drawing
showing foundations penetrating the voids of a
disused quarry

and that the element of "choice" that composition entails contradicts such a holistic view.

It would hardly be an exaggeration to say that the reaction against modernism in the last fifteen years or so is a symptom of the rejection of the claims of this idealism, with its insistence on the indivisibility and inevitability of cultural and technical development. Seen in this perspective, the dichotomy represented by *composizione/projettazione* or *composition/system* still carries a great deal of ideological meaning. *Composition* has been variously interpreted throughout the history of criticism, and there are good reasons why it should be reinterpreted for today.

Notes

1 It should be stressed, however, that in the figure/concept dichotomy implied by classical doctrine, the concept is not so abstract nor the figure so dependent as the romantics tended to assert.

2 An instance of this is the influence of Konrad Fiedler's ideas on the teaching course at the Bauhaus.

3 Laszlo Moholy-Nagy, *Von Material zu Architektur* (Munich, 1929); quoted in Reyner Banham, *Theory and Design in the First Machine Age* (London: Architectural Press, 1960), p. 317.

4 Ibid.

5 This process is well documented in Jean-Louis Cohen, "Le Corbusier and the Mystique of the U.S.S.R." *Oppositions* 23 (Winter 1981): 85.

6 Quatremère de Quincy, "Composition," in *Dictionnaire historique d'architecture* (Paris, 1832).

7 David Van Zanten, "Architectural Composition at the Ecole des Beaux-Arts from Charles Percier to Charles Garnier," in *The Architecture of the Ecole des Beaux-Arts*, ed. Arthur Drexler (New York: Museum of Modern Art, 1977), p. 112. Van Zanten gives *distribution* as a further precursor of the word *composition*, but this had quite a different meaning; see Quatremère de Quincy, "Distribution," in *Dictionnaire*.

8 Howard Robertson, *The Principles of Architectural Composition* (London, 1924) and *Modern Architectural Design* (London, 1932).

9 Leon Battista Alberti, *Della Pittura*, II.

10 Leon Battista Alberti, *De Re Aedificatoria*, IX, 5.

11 François Blondel, *Cours d'architecture enseigné dans l'académie royale d'architecture* (Paris, 1675–83).

12 Paul Frankl's classic distinction between an additive Renaissance and a subtractive Baroque, while not absolutely wrong, requires qualification.

13 Lionel Gossman, *Mediaevalism and the Ideologies of the Enlightenment* (Baltimore: Johns Hopkins University Press, 1968), p. 351.

14 Novalis, *Oeuvres complètes*, ed. A. Guerne (Paris, 1975); quoted in Tzvetan Todorov, *Theories of the Symbol* (Ithaca: Cornell University Press, 1984), p. 169.

15 Todorov, *Theories of the Symbol*, p. 169.

16 F. W. J. Schelling, *Sämmtliche Werke* (Stuttgart and Augsburg), 7, p. 302, quoted in Todorov, *Theories of the Symbol*, p. 169.

17 For the controversy between Raoul-Rochette on the one hand, and Lassus, Viollet-le-Duc, and the *Annales archéologiques* on the other, see Nikolaus Pevsner, *Some Architectural Writers of the Nineteenth Century* (Oxford: Clarendon Press, 1972), pp. 201–2.

18 M. H. Abrams, *The Mirror and the Lamp* (Oxford: Oxford University Press, 1953), p. 186.

Rationalism: A Philosophical Concept in Architecture

From Classical Rationalism to the Enlightenment:
The Search for Beauty

There is a common-sense view that divides mental activities into the scientific, depending on reason, and the artistic, depending on feeling or intuition. Such a simple dichotomy fails to take account of both the role that intuition plays in scientific thought and the role that the judgment-forming intellect plays in artistic creation. Nevertheless, the distinction contains an element of truth—less as a way of distinguishing between science and art than as a way of distinguishing between different aspects of the artistic process.

Of all the arts, architecture is the one in which it is least possible to exclude the idea of rationality. A building has to satisfy pragmatic and constructional criteria, which circumscribe, even if they do not determine, the field within which the imagination of the architect works. Therefore the degree to which architecture can be said to be rational depends less on the presence or absence of "rational" criteria than on the importance attributed to these criteria within the total process of architectural design and within particular ideologies. The "rational" in architecture never exists in isolation. It is not an art-historical category like neoclassicism. It is one side of a complex system that can be ex-

Originally published in *Das Abenteuer der Ideen: Architektur und Philosophie seit der Industriellen Revolution*, ed. Claus Baldus (Berlin: Internationale Bauausstellung, 1987).

pressed only in terms of a series of more or less homologous oppositions: reason/feeling, order/disorder, necessity/freedom, universal/particular, and so on.

But having made this initial distinction, we are immediately faced with another. The definition of the "rational" in architecture has not remained constant throughout history. We are dealing not with a simple, static concept, but with one that has varied according to the constellation of ideas dominating particular historical phases. These changes of meaning are dependent on changes in ideology and cannot be considered independently of either economic and social factors or philosophical ideas.

As a preliminary step in the definition of architectural rationalism, it is necessary to note the sense in which the term is used in the history of philosophy. In philosophy the primary distinction is that between rationalism and empiricism, or reason and experience. While the opposition reason/feeling cannot be reduced to these philosophical categories, there is nonetheless a relation between them. In both cases *reason* implies the intervention of rule or law between the direct experience of the world and any *praxis* or *techné* such as architecture. It is this notion—that architecture is the result of the application of general rules, established by the operation of reason—that may be taken as the most general definition of rationalism in architecture.

The conflict between rationalism and empiricism is one between two concepts of knowledge (or science), that define it as *a priori* or *a posteriori*. To the extent that knowledge is held to be *a priori*, empirical knowledge appears to be random, unfounded, and subject to contingency. To the extent that knowledge is held to be *a posteriori*, the terms are reversed and it is *a priori* knowledge that becomes unsure and dependent on authority, received ideas, or habit. The history of architectural theory during the last two hundred years has been the history of the conflict between these two concepts of architectural knowledge. But more than this; the dominance of one or the other has determined the role ascribed to those other mental processes that cannot be subsumed under the operation of reason or science. When discussing rationalism in architecture, therefore, we are discussing two sets of varying relationships: those that come from different concepts of knowledge itself, and those that come from the distinction between knowledge and intuition or feeling.

The rationalist philosophy of the seventeenth century, which we take here as represented by Descartes, Spinoza, and Leibniz, absorbed within its system the traditional view that there are innate ideas and that "science" is a fundamentally *a priori* enterprise based on these ideas. Innate ideas must be thought of as implanted by God, and, as such, they may be enshrined in a wisdom that has been revealed to mankind in the past and that constitutes valid authority. Knowledge gained by experience and induction has, ultimately, to be measured against this authority.

Cartesian rationalism did not abandon this tradition, but it inaugurated a search for clarity of concept, rigor of deduction, and intuitional certainty of basic principles. This is reflected in seventeenth-century academic artistic theory, of which Nicolas Boileau-Despréaux's *L'art poétique*, Jean-Philippe Rameau's *Traité de l'harmonie réduite à ses principes naturels*, and François Blondel's *Cours d'architecture* may be taken as examples.

The principles enunciated in these works were themselves based on an older body of ideas. When, in the late fifteenth century, architecture was first constituted as a separate branch of science, an important part of the knowledge forming this science depended on the authority of the ancients and the precepts found in the only surviving ancient architectural treatise, that of Vitruvius. At the same time, architectural theory began to be inscribed within a general artistic doctrine derived from Aristotle, Horace, and Cicero, on the one hand, and neoplatonism on the other. The most important component of this doctrine was the idea that art was an imitation of nature, and that the art of the ancients, being derived from this law, was also worthy of imitation. Thus, nature was chiefly approachable through the authority of the ancients. This notion of authority is closely linked to the seventeenth-century doctrine of *a priori* knowledge and innate ideas.

One of the sources of the concept of imitation can be found in Aristotle's *Physics*. He says:

If a house were one of the things provided by nature, it would be the same as it is now when produced by art. And if natural phenomena were produced not only by nature but also by art, they would in this case come into being through art in the same way as they do in nature. . . . In short, art either completes the process that nature is unable to work out fully, or it imitates nature.[1]

Here we see two ideas which, to the modern mind, seem quite different, if not contradictory: the idea that architecture and other artifacts are extensions of nature's laws, and the idea that this entails a process of imitation or representation. In fact, throughout the eighteenth and nineteenth centuries there is a progressive separation between these two ideas and the concept of architecture becomes split between its constructive and "scientific" and its representational and "artistic" functions, *reason* being reserved for the former and *feeling*, or *sentiment*, for the latter.

Such a split, however, would have been inconceivable to the classical mind. Access to the truth and beauty was by way of laws that were already inscribed—

however obscurely—in nature. Truth was the revelation of what already existed, and if it depended on revelation it must equally be based on truths already revealed to previous men. All truth was therefore a re-presentation. This view is still found in certain writers until the end of the eighteenth century. The English architect John Wood the Elder held that the *science* of architecture was its speculative or metaphysical part, while the *art* of architecture was the knowledge of its specific causes and its application to human uses.[2] It is the final cause that gives meaning to architecture, not the efficient cause or the solutions to specific problems. The distinction we find here between science and art is the opposite of the one generally made today; science for Wood belonged to the realm of metaphysics and art to the realm of the practical and the contingent. Quatremère de Quincy is equally adamant that architecture should imitate the *idea* of nature. This imitation results in a building having a certain "character," which may be of three kinds—essential, relative, and accidental—according to whether one is imitating nature in her more generic and timeless aspects or in her more specific and momentary aspects.[3] (The idea of character comes from the theory of genres in Aristotle's *Poetics*, but Quatremère turns it into something rather neoplatonic).

But a new attitude was developing within the ethos of seventeenth-century rationalism, which emphasized the role that both empirical science and individual intelligence played in the discovery of truth and which tended to throw doubt on the status of *a priori* knowledge and innate ideas, as much as on the authority of the ancients or of the Bible. The quarrel between the "ancients" and the "moderns" gave rise to an increasingly critical dispute as to which architectural rules belonged to the realm of innate ideas and which belonged to the realm of empirical experience. The "lawful" now becomes split between what was eternal and absolute and what was customary—the latter coming increasingly under the guidance of "taste."

This split is exemplified in both architectural and musical theory. In architecture, Claude Perrault attacked the classical doctrine of the orders, claiming that the rules of proportion were based solely on custom.[4] In music, there was disagreement between the followers of Gioseffe Zarlino (1517–90), who had insisted on the mathematical basis for acceptable chords, and those of Vincenzo Galilei (1533–91), who had said that what was beautiful could be decided only by the ear.

In the face of this problem, it became the aim of the eighteenth century to reconcile a rationalistic *a priorism* with taste or subjective judgment and to show that the constitution of the individual human being tends toward a harmony with Natural Law. As Charles-Etienne Briseaux said:

Nature always acts with the same wisdom and in a uniform manner . . . from which it can be concluded that the pleasure of the ear and the eye consists of the perfection of harmonic concordance as being analogous to our own constitutions . . . and that this principle resides not only in music but in all the productions of the arts.[5]

In Laugier's *Essai sur l'architecture* of 1753, the rules of good architecture are presented as self-evident to the uncorrupted mind and eye; *a priori* reason is confirmed by empirical experience and by sensation. In this way, untutored reason confirms the truths of the earliest architecture and no longer depends on the guidance of particular antique models. But reason and truth were still tied to the purification of the tradition, of which more or less imperfect models already existed. Just as it was the task of the painter or sculptor, in classical and neoclassical doctrine, to imitate the idea lying behind the imperfect appearances of nature, so it was the task of the architect to uncover the types lying concealed in the manifold, but imperfect, examples presented by the history of architecture. Architecture is treated exactly as if it were a natural phenomenon. Even Carlo Lodoli, whose functionalism *avant la lettre* has often been mistaken for a pure empiricism, adhered to a concept of architectural ornament in which there is a clear distinction between what is normative and typical and what is due to "accidental" cultural differences.[6] The Enlightenment may have wanted to replace *l'esprit du système* by *l'esprit systématique*, in order to free practice from the domination of authority and received ideas, but its aim was still to discover the universal and unchanging laws underlying empirical experience. A building such as Soufflot's Sainte-Geneviève, uniting "the noble decoration of the Greeks and the lightness of the Gothic architects,"[7] and the rationalism of a Lodoli or a Laugier both pointed to the need to free architecture from the arbitrary and tasteless rules to which it had succumbed under the Baroque and bring it back to nature, whose laws were simple and eternal.

This project was similar in many ways to the Grammarians' search for the universal and rational laws of language.[8] Architecture also was a rational "language," subject to the variations of character demanded by climate, custom, and decorum, but capable, nevertheless, of being reduced by the exercise of reason to a universal system, whose laws even genius could not escape. The eighteenth century is marked by the opposition reason/caprice, reason alone being capable of discerning universal truths. But this *reason* is now in alliance with subjective experience; empirical experience is no longer set in opposition to a reason that has been implanted in us by God and that constitutes an unquestioned authority. It is used as a supplementary proof of the existence of Natural Law.

Utilitarian and Eclectic Rationalism:
The Search for Utility

With the growth of utilitarianism the structure of thought on which the alliance between rationalism and classicism depended became increasingly tenuous. "Scientific" reason became increasingly directed to instrumental efficacy rather than metaphysics. Efficient causes replaced final causes. There was now no theory that could withstand the growth of caprice and eclecticism, or the proliferation of what Quatremère called "accidental character." J.-N.-L. Durand, though still working within the formal language of classicism, justified a rational architecture purely on grounds of economics and utility.[9] The efforts of architects and theorists like Durand, Legrand, Thomas Hope, and Schinkel were now directed to an irenic eclecticism which would select, in a system of combinations and permutations, appropriate stylistic elements from the panorama of history or from buildings of a utilitarian nature. There were now as many "architectures" (the word is Legrand's) as there were times and peoples; classicism was reduced to a specific tradition (admittedly "our own") whose use was justified purely by convention. At the end of his book *Essai sur l'histoire générale de l'architecture* of 1800, Legrand puts the rhetorical question:

Can we not arrive at the end [of a modern architecture] by borrowing from all the genres what each has of the reasonable and the exquisite, so as to compose a modern style appropriate to the climate, customs, materials . . . and rules of decorum of each country, and which will be the happy result of our knowledge of the art of building among all the peoples? [10]

Thomas Hope expresses the same opinion:

No one seems yet to have conceived the . . . wish . . . of only borrowing of every former style in architecture, whatever it might present of the useful and ornamental, of the scientific and tasteful . . . and then composing an architecture which . . . grown on our own soil, and in harmony with our own climate, institutions and habits . . . should truly deserve the appellation of "our own." [11]

But however much these sentiments might seem to anticipate the "organic society" of romanticism and the Gothic revival, they still adhere to eighteenth-century notions of decorum and to that conception of "mechanical composition" which, ever since 1800, had been virulently attacked by the German romantics.[12]

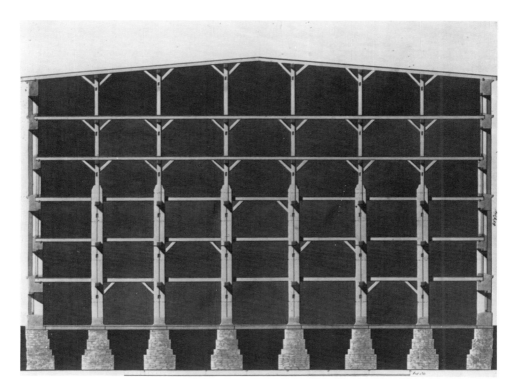

School of David Gilly, Warehouse, section,
c. 1800

Structural and Organic Rationalism:
The Search for Authenticity

From the second half of the eighteenth century onward the conceptual split between architecture as construction and architecture as representation had begun to undermine seriously the unitary doctrine of classicism. But a weak form of classical doctrine nonetheless persisted, in which it was possible to think of the use of different styles as permissible within the classical notions of character and decorum.

The development of a rationalism based on the logic of structure took place chiefly in France, where, as far back as the seventeenth century, architects had recognized in Gothic architecture a rational constructive principle. The structural rationalists of the late eighteenth century did not reject classicism; they sought to subject it to more stringent functional analysis in terms of the new science of the strength of materials and in terms of use.[13] This tradition continued well into the nineteenth century, even after the impact of Comtian positivism. The belief, characteristic of the positivists, that science provides us with the only valid knowledge and that facts are its only objects, was quite compatible with a form of idealism that promoted all that was not reducible to experimental science to a vaguely neoclassical realm of "Beauty." This view was expressed by Léonce Reynard, a prominent teacher of classical-rationalist persuasion in the mid-nineteenth century:

Although I believe that considerations of a scientific kind must enter into the study of the forms of our buildings, I am far from thinking that they cover everything. That which touches the intimate essence of art is felt, not explained.[14]

For Reynard, classicism was a set of broadly defined formal principles onto which an architecture appropriate to a scientific age could be grafted. Certain historical forms had reached a sort of perfection through evolution and should not be discarded (echoes of this notion will still be found in Le Corbusier). The categories into which Reynard divided architectural values—utility, order and simplicity, and character—were similar to those that had been suggested by Durand half a century earlier.

The last representative of this tradition, César Daly, founder of the *Revue générale d'architecture*, defined architectural rationalism as follows:

1. Architecture is ornamented structure.

2. Architectural forms require rational justification and must derive their laws from science.

3. The task of the rationalist school is to reconcile architecture with modern science and technology.

4.   Once the alliance of architecture and reason is accomplished, the next step is the alliance of architecture and sentiment.[15]

Among practicing architects, the same syncretism between modern technique and classicism is often apparent. For example, in the Bibliothèque Sainte-Geneviève, Henri Labrouste does not allow his interest in iron structure to interfere with his idea—derived from classical theory—about the correct external form of a public monument.

This debate, however, took a different form among the Gothic revivalists. According to them, Gothic architecture was not a style that could be used eclectically, as a way of eliciting literary associations *within* the classical definition of "character"; it should be seen as an *alternative* tradition to that of classicism. The difference between the Gothic revivalists and the classical eclectics was that for the former structure itself became the basis of architectural meaning. Ornament and "representation" were now thought of as emerging from the structure of a building, rather than as arbitrary clothing that could be added to it. It followed that, of the three kinds of character described by Quatremère, only the first—essential character—was kept.

The chief spokesman for this school of thought and possibly the most influential architectural writer of the nineteenth century was Viollet-le-Duc.[16] For him technique becomes the basis for an architecture that is rational in its very essence. He sees in Gothic architecture a constructional principle that should become the methodological paradigm of a future architecture. In spite of a predominance of restorations in Viollet's oeuvre and his nostalgia for medieval culture, his writings exhibit the same adherence to positivism as those of the opposing school of classical eclectics, and an even stronger belief in the open-ended progress of mankind, which, it was supposed, would follow in the wake of the Industrial Revolution. But for Viollet the history of architecture is a continuous technological development, which excludes the possibility of repeating the "perfect" forms derived from antiquity. The morphology of architecture is no longer determined by a taxonomy of external and historical *forms*, but by a system of underlying *functions*. "That which is generally regarded as a matter of true art, namely symmetry, the apparent form, is quite a secondary consideration."[17]

This "evolutionary" rationalism, which tied architecture to an implacable and objective historical destiny, was combined with a subjective moralism. The principles of Gothic architecture were both rational *and* moral. In a brilliant analysis of Viollet's writings, Philippe Junod shows that he is constantly fluctuating between an objective and a subjective viewpoint. On the one hand, reason is opposed to sentiment, logic to fantasy, system to instinct, in a way that allies him to a rationalist tradition extending, *mutatis mutandis,* from Descartes to Comte; on the other, sincerity, honesty, and truth are opposed to pretense, falsehood, and lies. In this circular argument, Viollet appeals to subjective feeling to justify the rational, and to the rational to justify subjective feeling.[18]

What are those "laws" which enable Viollet to fluctuate with such apparent inconsistency between a negative and a positive evaluation of subjective sentiment? They are the Laws of Nature, imperative equally to the head and the heart, to the objective world and to feeling. In discussing the relation between the parts of a building and the whole, Viollet says, "Just as when one sees the leaf of a plant, one deduces from it the entire plant: from the bone of an animal, the entire animal, so, in seeing a profile, one deduces the members of architecture, and from the members the entire monument."[19] There was nothing particularly new in this analogy; Denis Diderot had already suggested that zoology offered the artist a typical example of functional coherence.[20] But by the mid-nineteenth century the argument had deepened. Viollet (like Gottfried Semper) could adduce the example of Cuvier's "functional" taxonomy of animal species; moreover, he was following in the footsteps of German romanticism. His organic analogy is not far from that expressed by A. W. Schlegel in his *Dramatic Lectures:*

66

The form is mechanical when . . . it is imparted to a material merely as an accidental addition, without relation to its nature. . . . Organic form, on the other hand, is innate; it unfolds itself from within and acquires its definiteness simultaneously with the total development of the germ. . . . All genuine forms are organic, i.e., determined by the content of the work of art. In a word, art is nothing but a significant exterior, the speaking physiognomy of everything . . . which bears witness to its hidden nature.[21]

Unless we recognize this romantic and "organicist" aspect of Viollet, which is integral to his interpretation of Gothic, it is difficult to explain his influence on the twentieth-century avant-garde, on Art Nouveau vitalism, and on architects of the Chicago school. Louis Sullivan's theory of an "organic" architecture (taken over later by Frank Lloyd Wright) is derived partly from Viollet and partly from the German romantics (presumably via Coleridge and the American transcendentalists), and it is clearly expressed in the statement: "It is the pervading law of all things, organic and inorganic, of all things human and superhuman, of all true manifestations of the head, the heart and the soul, that life is recognizable in its expression, that form always follows function. This is the law."[22]

It is evident that a strict line cannot be drawn, in the nineteenth century, between positivistic rationalism and a romantic organicism, with its emphasis of the moral imperative that underlies the need to conform to the laws of nature. But in this essay we cannot pursue that other thread that leads from Viollet-le-

Duc through Art Nouveau to organicism and expressionism because it would lead us away from the main stream of the twentieth-century avant-garde, in which the theory of organic form was assimilated to ideas of an analytical and mechanistic kind, embracing the machine, rather than opposing it.

Rationalism and the Twentieth-century Avant-Garde:
The Search for Transparency

It has often been argued that it was not until the twentieth century that positivism and the structural rationalism of the nineteenth century bore fruit. If the law of historical evolution and progress was to be demonstrated, architecture would have finally to sever its ties with past styles and draw its meaning and its language exclusively from the objective conditions of technique and program. It was not until the end of the nineteenth century that certain architects began to put these principles into operation. Among these, H. P. Berlage and Otto Wagner were outstanding in the way in which they were able to transform their stylistic inheritance (Gothic revival and neo-classical, respectively) by the application of rational constructional principles. Those two paradigmatic "halls" of the early twentieth century, the Amsterdam Exchange and the Post Office Savings building in Vienna, both assimilate the nineteenth-century exhibition or railway shed to sociocultural programs and embed them in an architecture which, though recognizably traditional in overall form, tries to develop a new kind of ornament derived from construction.

However, although the craftsmanlike principles embodied in these buildings were incorporated into the doctrine of the twentieth-century avant-garde, the rationalism of the "modern movement" cannot be understood in these terms alone. Twentieth-century rationalism differs radically from that of the nineteenth century, and to understand this difference it is necessary to analyze it in terms of three concepts: *logical atomism, functionalism,* and *formalism,* which, while not absolutely new, now take an entirely new form.

Logical Atomism

Logic was stressed in positivistic thought, but we have seen that for Viollet-le-Duc there was always a passage from logic, via technique, to subjective feeling and organic nature. Viollet had talked about the machine as a paradigm for architecture, but for him mechanization did not imply any change in the relation between the components of architecture and the building as a whole. Iron could be substituted for wood or stone, but his substitution, though it entailed substantial formal transformations, depended on the fact that these materials had analogous properties and could still be "worked" in a craftsmanlike way. It was

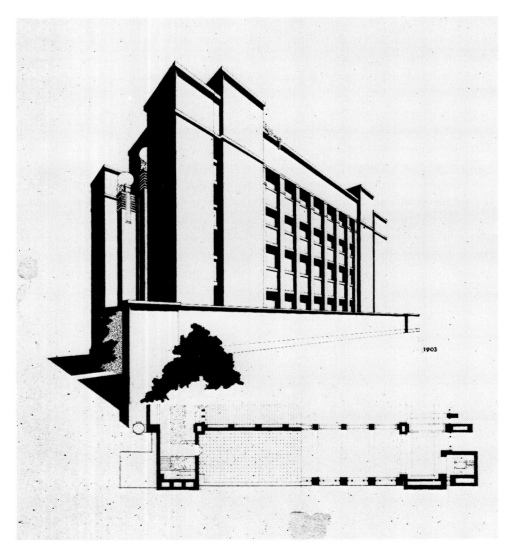

1903

Frank Lloyd Wright, Larkin Company building,
Buffalo, New York, 1903, perspective and partial
plan

precisely such linking of "logic" and "technique" that enabled Viollet to see architecture as a continuous process of evolution, whose principles remained constant, even if their material embodiment changed.

A series of developments in aesthetic theory, in philosophy, in construction, and in production in the late nineteenth and early twentieth centuries intervened to alter quite radically this fundamentally traditional conception of architecture. There can be no question of assigning causes and effects; we will merely juxtapose certain parallel developments that have *prima facie* similarities.

The constructional and productive conditions of twentieth-century architecture were laid down in the second half of the nineteenth century by engineers using cast and wrought iron in the construction of bridges, greenhouses, train stations, and market and exhibition structures. In all these constructions it was possible to develop pragmatic and analytical methods with the minimum of interference from architectural ideology. A crucial example is Paxton's Crystal Palace of 1851, where for the first time and within the ambit of a typically English pragmatism, division of labor and standardization of tools and materials became an essential part of the design concept. In the tower that Gustav Eiffel built for the Paris exhibition of 1889, in addition to these productive procedures, empirico-mathematical methods of design are used to produce forms of novel transparency and dynamism. A further development of construction is found later in the bridges of Robert Maillart, in which a completely new concept of reinforced concrete planes is developed.

The first application on a substantial scale of these new kinds of empirical procedure to architecture was the introduction of the steel frame in multistory office buildings in Chicago in the 1880s. In the steel frame the elements of construction are determined more by the needs of the production process than by the sort of constructional "logic" which formed the basis of Viollet's philosophy. The frame introduces a generalized system that minimizes differences precisely when Viollet would have maximized them; for example, the differences between supporting and supported elements, and their point of connection. The forms that result are closer to Cartesian abstraction than to the quasi- "organic" laws of material and the visual expression of these laws.

There are broad parallels between such pragmatic developments and certain contemporary developments in philosophy, notably Bertrand Russell's theories of *logical constructionism* and *logical atomism*, which he started to develop in about 1900. In his theory of logical constructionism, Russell tried to show that all entities which were problematic from the point of view of empirical experience and common sense could be reduced to (or "constructed" out of) simpler and nonproblematic entities: "The supreme maxim in scientific philosophising is this: wherever possible logical constructions are to be substituted for inferred

Auguste and Gustav Perret, Apartment building at 25 bis rue Franklin, 1903

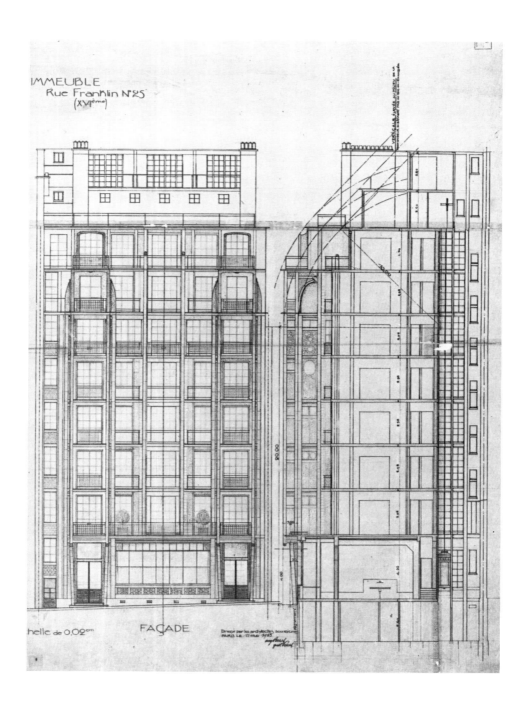

70

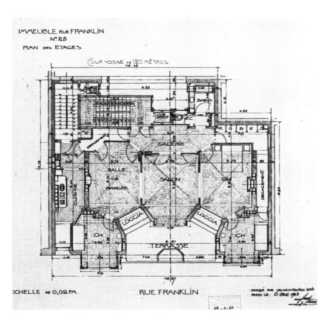

Auguste and Gustav Perret, Apartment building at 25 bis rue Franklin, typical floor plan

72

Otto Wagner, Post Office Savings Bank, Vienna,
1903–6, main hall

Hendrik Petrus Berlage, Amsterdam Exchange,
Produce Exchange, 1898–1903, detail of western
wall

entities." The theory of logical atomism, which Russell developed slightly later, was an attempt to give metaphysical status to this purely epistemological principle by postulating an ideal, empirically-based, language which would correspond to the structure of reality.

- The world consists of elementary entities possessing only elementary properties and connected through elementary relations.
- Our scientific world view has to be composed analogically out of elementary propositions.

The paradox of this project is that in order to satisfy empirical truth requirements, the world has to be subjected to a purely formal analysis and divested of all immediacy of meaning. It attempts to reduce all mental operations to those appropriate for the physical sciences.

There is a strong parallel between this view and that of the founders of the modern movement in the second decade of the twentieth century, who similarly wished to break down the inherited figures of art and architecture into their irreducible elements. Whether these elements are thought of as "formal" (as with Kandinsky, Mondrian, and the de Stijl movement) or as "constructive" (as in the Russian avant-garde), they constitute a lexicon of irreducible entities connected to each other by means of elementary relations. As in Russell's "constructionism," totalities are replaced by simples, whose meaning is immanent and self-evident.

This elementarization can certainly be thought of as an impoverishment of the meanings carried by cultural convention. But it should be stressed that this was not the interpretation given to it in avant-garde artistic circles, where, on the contrary, it was construed as a means of attaining more profound—because more primitive—meanings and of distancing the artist from a "degenerate" bourgeois conception of art.

These tendencies had started before the events we have been describing. They can be seen, for example, in Impressionist and Post-Impressionist painting, where the manifold of perception is analyzed into, and reconstructed out of, atomic units. They can also be seen in German formalist, neo-Kantian aesthetics, from Herbart to Fiedler,[23] in which a logic of artistic apperception is developed. Such developments must be considered as part of a "rationalist" program, insofar as they seek to apply the methodology of science to the analysis of subjective experience. It is from the inheritors of this analytical tradition in painting—principally Cubism—that the architectural modernists of the 1920s drew their formal inspiration, whatever their other sources, positivistic or metaphysical.

An even more direct connection with the philosophy of logical atomism, however, may perhaps be seen in the work of Adolf Loos, whose *Raumplan Analysen* were begun around the turn of the century. Here the space of the house is built up out of atomic "rooms," each with its own specificity. A further example is the house that Ludwig Wittgenstein built for his sister in 1926 in collaboration with the architect Paul Engelmann. In this house all the elements are redefined in terms of elementary functions and seem to reflect Wittgenstein's picture theory of language, given in the *Tractatus logico-philosophicus* (and developed under the influence of Russell), according to which there is a one-to-one relationship between sentences and things. This house belongs equally to the spirit of the 1920s avant-garde and to Wittgenstein's own philosophical preoccupations; nothing could express more clearly his dictum "The meaning is the use."

The insistence on "use value" in the architecture of Loos and Wittgenstein links the idea of logical atomism to the notion of "function."

Functionalism

The idea, fundamental to the modern movement, that there is an overriding causal relation between functions and forms in architecture is part of a tradition going back to Vitruvius. Until the end of the eighteenth century, as we have seen, this idea was closely united with the idea of imitation in the sense given by Aristotle. But in the first half of the nineteenth century, under the influence of romanticism and historicism, it became associated with the notion of genetic development. An *inner necessity* took place of *analogy* as the generator of forms expressive of the program or the structure of a building. This "inner necessity" was capable of either an idealist interpretation (an invisible spirit giving direction to material causality) or a "scientific" interpretation (based on efficient causes and empirical investigation).

By the end of the nineteenth century the sense in which the word "function" is used in different disciplines has lost much of its idealist content. In mathematics, for example, a function is no longer a relation between a variable and a known, fixed object; it is a relation between two variables. According to Ernst Mach, the notion of function should replace that of cause. When science gathers various elements into one equation, each element becomes a *function* of the others; the dependence among elements becomes reciprocal, and the relation between cause and effect becomes reversible.[24]

Such a notion of function, with its implication of a system that is independent of external "values," is closely related to the functionalist anthropology of Bronislaw Malinowski. According to Malinowski's hypothesis, societies are to be seen as self-organizing systems, and the *function* of an element is the part it plays in maintaining the system. As Malinowski said, "The functional view . . . insists upon the principle that in every type of civilization, every custom, material object, idea and belief, fulfills some vital function . . . within the working whole."[25] The circularity of this argument is evident; the system is defined as the sum of the facts, while the "fact" is defined as what is relevant to the system.

Something analogous to this view is found in the idea of a "functional" architecture. According to this, there must be no interference, in the design or evaluation of a building, from preconceived notions about what "architecture" is. It should be defined solely in terms of elements interacting with each other *within* the (empirically founded) system, which, in turn can only be defined as the sum of these elements.

The *neue Sachlichkeit* group of modern architects present, in their theory, an extreme example of this kind of "functionalism." When Hannes Meyer defined architecture as *function x economics* he was trying to reduce architecture to an absolutely primitive system excluding all *a priori* "values."[26] But of course the nature of this system was already given by his own arbitrary restriction to the relevant facts: those, like structure, economy, and fundamental "needs," which could be empirically tested by the "scientific" method. In a fully axiomaticized field of knowledge such as mathematics, such arbitrary limitations are justified, and indeed essential. But in an affective and ideological field like architecture, their rigid application can be explained only by ideological motives that are the invisible agents of their self-exclusion.

The term *functional*, as used in modern architecture, was colored by this arbitrary limitation as to what could be logically deduced or empirically verified. The results, instead of being understood as aspects of a purely formal operation, as they are in mathematics, were taken as objectively true descriptions of the real world.

A similar situation pertained to "functionalism" in anthropology, where the recording of empirically observable behavior was considered to be the only way of arriving at truth statements about a particular society.

In the 1940s, in anthropology and somewhat later in architecture, a structuralist critique was developed, whose purpose was to demonstrate that there was no necessary correlation between forms and structures on the one hand and "functions" and "behavior patterns" on the other. Forms, it was claimed, were independent of the empirical situations which lent them "meaning" at any one time or place.

Formalism

We can define formalism as that type of thought which stresses rule-governed relationships rather than relationships of cause and effect. According to this definition, formalism is related to a purely mathematical definition of function. It studies the structures of given fields independently of what exists outside those fields; it is concerned with the "how" of things, not with the "why." This seems to be characteristic of late-nineteenth-century and early-twentieth-century thought in widely different disciplines—philosophy, mathematics, art and architecture.

We have already mentioned this approach in connection with nineteenth-century German aesthetic theory. It can also be seen, somewhat later, in the history of art. Here a formalist approach restricts the object of study to the formal structures of works of art and avoids discussion of what these works have been held to "mean" at particular historical periods. In the same way, it looks for a logic of historical change in the specifically artistic problems that have faced artists at different times, rather than seeing them as the (undemonstrable) result of external historical events. The art historians Franz Wickhoff, Aloïs Riegl, and Heinrich Wölfflin were representative of this point of view. All were strongly influenced by Konrad Fiedler's theory of "pure visibility," and all, in turn, influenced the intellectual atmosphere of the artistic avant-garde of the early twentieth century.

While one of the aims of formalist art history was to break the hold of normative classical aesthetics, these aims could only be achieved by establishing more general norms which would apply to all art, of whatever period. It thus tended toward the establishment of ahistorical laws, and in doing so resembled classical theory itself. Formalist art theory concentrated on the "how" of art because it rejected the kind of "why" explanations always given to justify a particular system of values (or a particular style). But classical doctrine also concentrated on the "how" (the rules of good poetry and of rhetoric, etc.) precisely because it *accepted,* without question, a particular system of values.

The formalist tendencies of the twentieth-century avant-garde therefore contradicted the historicist interpretations of modern architecture given by Viollet-le-Duc and his followers. Instead of seeing architecture as continuously developing according to a historical law of technical and social evolution, they carry the implication that modern architecture is a radical break with history—that it has reached a threshold which enables it to give form to the eternal laws of aesthetics. In this way it can be seen as a type of classicism, but one which rejects the specific, historically determined forms of the classical style. This view was, nonetheless, closely connected to developments in constructional techniques, which were seen as freeing the architect from those technical constraints that had previously tied architectural aesthetics to particular times and particular craft traditions.

One of the first architects explicitly to connect an industrialized architecture to classicism was Hermann Muthesius, who saw in it the means of arriving at a typology of architectural forms corresponding to universal laws of aesthetic perception. The rationalization of building in terms of factory production would recreate, at a more abstract level, the very artistic traditions and cultural values it had helped to destroy.[27]

In the 1920s most of the avant-garde architects began to accept the replacement of craft by the machine as the price architecture had to pay in order to tackle the urgent social tasks presented to it. But, although this involved a certain simplification of masses and the stressing of the typical over the individual, its incipient classicism was overshadowed by elementarist and montage-like compositional principles that denied the formal hierarchies of the classical system. This was particularly true of the so-called *neue Sachlichkeit* architects working in the Weimar Republic—Hannes Meyer, Ernst May, Mart Stam, and Hans Schmidt, among others.

There is, in the work of these architects, and especially in the city layouts by Ludwig Hilbersheimer, an extreme schematicism, which transposes diagrams resulting from purely analytical operations into objects of the real, perceptual world. This is a primitive kind of formalism which halts the process of abstraction midway, as it were, without allowing it to work toward an adequate image.

In the work of Le Corbusier and Mies van der Rohe, however, this schematic formalism was combined with more overt classical tendencies. Le Corbusier's classicism, in particular, was quite explicit and was based on a rather generalized acceptance of the French classical tradition. In the greater part of his work he was concerned with reconciling the classical idea of an *a priori* artistic order with the notion of continuous progress he had inherited from the historicist and positivist traditions. His drawing of the Dom-ino frame was the first demonstration of a dialectical principle that was to dominate all his subsequent work. Here, the concrete frame carries all the certainty of a Cartesian *a priori*. Within this frame, the volumes and equipment of the house can be independently arranged, according to practical needs. The organization of these needs is supposed to follow an empirical necessity whose laws are as rigorous as those of the Platonic frame and its implied cubic envelope (though, in fact, it is precisely here that the invention of the architect/artist comes into play, with all its freedom of metaphorical allusion). The dialogue between the frame and its infill is made apparent by means of Cubist techniques of spatial simultaneity, themselves made possible by new constructional techniques.

Le Corbusier's architecture gives artistic expression to the conflict between the two traditions of rationalism we have traced: the *a priori* and the empirical. On the one hand, we find those "clear and distinct ideas" which, translated from a Cartesian metaphysics into the sensuous objects of art, had been promoted by French classical theorists from Boileau to Durand. On the other, we find the empirical and scientific ideas of positivism, which are expressed as the func-

Ludwig Hilberseimer, Project for a city of skyscrapers, 1924, east-west street

Giuseppe Terragni, Casa del Fascio, Como,
1934, rear perspective

tional, the accidental, and the contingent. Both are reducible to a typology: the first to those types which are inscribed in our very consciousness, the second to those types which are the result of a teleological evolution.

A formalism tending equally toward the classical is found in both Scandinavian and Italian modernism. In Scandinavia it is present in the work of Gunnar Asplund and the early work of Alvar Aalto—in both cases due to the existence of a strong tradition of neoclassicism dating from the first decade of the twentieth century.

In Italy this tendency is inseparable from the cultural demands of Fascism and the attempt to reconcile progressivist ideals with tradition. The example of Le Corbusier's architecture and writings was probably the most important single influence on the Italian avant-garde of the 1930s (the self-styled "rationalists" of Gruppo 7). In his book *Vers une architecture*, published in 1923, Le Corbusier had equated the products of modern technology, such as automobiles, with the Parthenon—each being presented as the result of an evolutionary process terminating in a perfect "type" form. This image enabled the Italian architects to reconcile the dynamic and mechanistic aspects of Futurism with the classical tradition.

Antonio Sant'Elia, in his *Città Nuova* of 1914, had synthesized ideas from Henri Sauvage and the Wagnerschule to produce the sublime image of a congested and mechanized modern city. If we compare the images in this book with a work of the rationalists, such as the Casa del Fascio by Giuseppe Terragni, and certain works by Eduardo Persico and Gino Pollini, we see that Sant'Elia's romantic expressionism has given way to a calm and timeless classicism. This classicism, however, lacks the stylistic iconography characteristic of the Novecento architects Giovanni Muzio and Marcello Piacentini. It is reduced to an abstract "framework" of deliberate neutrality.

Postmodernism:
The Search for Meaning

The modern movement of the 1920s was marked by an evangelical fervor which lent it all the attributes of a religious movement. As in all religious movements, its adherents had to pass through a *conversion* to a state of mind in which the smallest and most mundane aspects of life were transfigured. The rationalism of the twentieth-century avant-garde was enveloped by a dogmatic and idealistic antirationalism that could, perhaps, only survive in a pure form for a very short time.

Already in the 1930s a process of "liberalization" set in, which culminated in the 1950s. This liberalization did not abandon the rationalist position as a foun-

Adalberto Libera, Concourse for the urban reorganization of the beach at Castelfusano, 1933–
34, perspective

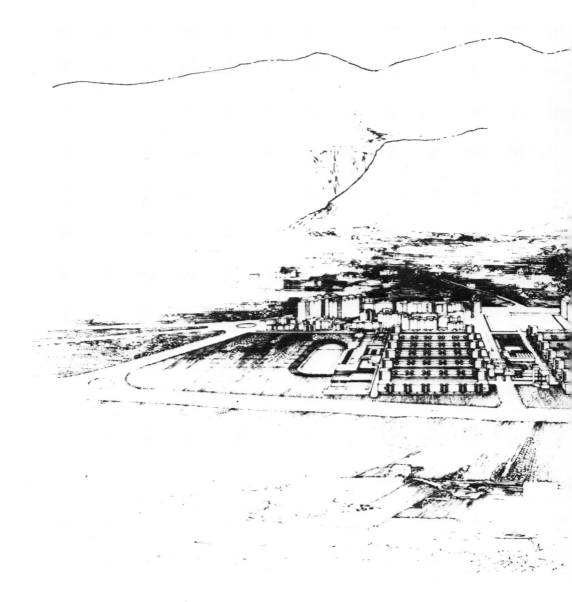

Vittorio Gregotti, Franco Amoroso, Salvatore
Bisogni, Hiromichi Matsui, and Franco Purini,
Zen Quarter, Palermo, 1970, perspective

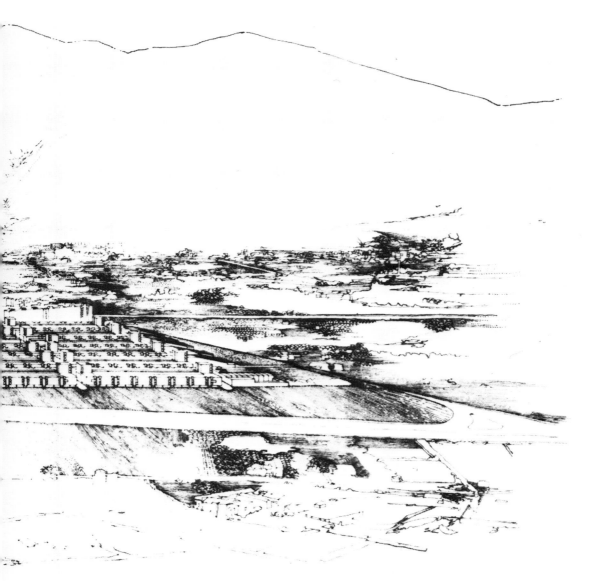

83

dation, but sought to "humanize" it. In the 1930s Le Corbusier began to intro-
duce natural materials and vernacular elements into his work, J. J. P. Oud, who
had been associated with the De Stijl movement, attempted to reintroduce ornament into his buildings, and Alvar Aalto developed a style that explicitly allowed room for "irrational" and "psychological" factors. After World War II this
process continued under the various rubrics of "neoempiricism," "brutalism,"
and "neorealism." At the same time, particularly in the United States, technical
development reached a stage at which it became possible to harness the rational/
constructive aspect of modernism to the ideological needs of real estate development, thus undermining modernism's utopian foundations.

None of these tendencies questioned the basic premises of modernist rationalism. They saw modernism as capable of gradually reforming itself from
within, so as to absorb those "humanistic" and pragmatic needs that had been
excluded from its original program.

A parallel development can perhaps be seen in developments within analytical philosophy. Wittgenstein's "language games," introduced in the *Philosophical
Investigations,* the "ordinary language" philosophy of J. L. Austin, and Karl Pop-
per's concept of the "open society," all, in various ways, relinquished the attempt to equate the processes of rational analysis with the real world.

In the mid 1960s, however, there was a powerful reaction in architectural discourse, which, instead of trying to reform architecture from within a specifically
modernist interpretation of rationalism, sought rather to redefine rationalism in
terms of an autonomous tradition of architecture. This movement originated in
the circle of young architects grouped around Ernesto Rogers, the editor of the
magazine *Casabella.* The specific transformation to which rationalism had been
subject in historical development were seen as secondary to, and dependent
upon, a deeper tradition according to which what is "rational" in architecture is
that which conserves architecture as a cultural discourse throughout history.
These ideas were based to a large extent on structural linguistics, which had
stressed the paradigmatic value of the typical and invariant structures underlying individual speech acts.

Although there is an evident historical connection between this view and the
formalistic aspects of modernism, they differ in one crucial respect. Modernist
formalism had assumed that architecture could be reduced to forms which cor-
responded to the structure of the human mind (*les constants humains*), whereas
the new formalism we are describing sees the invariant elements of architecture
as irreducible beyond the experience of architecture itself, as a social and cultural reality.

The implication of this view is that we should look upon the history of architecture—or at any rate a large segment of it—as if it were a continuous instant

in which thought and memory are coextensive. The model for such a view is Enlightenment thought, which looked on progress not as the unpredictable and open-ended development it was to become for positivism, but as the rational rearrangement and exploitation of existing material. According to such a view, the typological characteristics of a rational architecture are not those that are created by technology or by the specifically modern forms of social behavior, but those that persist through technological and social change and anchor us to a permanent image of man. There is a return to an eighteenth-century view of reason, as the faculty which is, itself, outside history: history provides reason with changing models of human achievement (in this case architectural) from which it is able freely to choose.

The architects who exemplify these attitudes most clearly are Giorgio Grassi and Aldo Rossi. The former emphasizes the more ontological and tectonic aspects of the rationalist tradition, while the latter stresses those subjective and poetic images to which it can give rise.[28] As part of a more general "postmodern" tendency, this type of rationalism must be seen as a defensive reaction to the current social conditions of production and consumption. It is not an accident that in both cases the output is small and deliberately modest in scale. We have reached a stage in social evolution in which the products of man's reason are increasingly divorced from the experience of making, constructing, or imagining. Talking, in 1894, of the distance between modern scientific conceptual thought and our capacity to reduce the world to sensuous images of order, Paul Valéry wrote:

Why is it that only a small part of the world can be so reduced? There is a moment when the figural becomes so complicated, or the event seems so new, that we must abandon the attempt to consider them as a whole, or to proceed with their translation into continuous values. At what point did our Euclids halt their apprehension of form? [29]

Nearly a hundred years later the problem has become all the more glaring. Can we still use the word *rationalism* in architecture in the sense that it has always been used despite all its changes of meaning: as the attempt to provide the sensuous analogue, the emblematic presence, of that reason which was once supposed to permeate the universe?

Notes

1 Aristotle, *Physics*, 199a, 15–19.

2 John Wood the Elder, *The Origin of Building, or the Plagiarism of the Heathens Detected* (London, 1741).

3 Quatremère de Quincy, "Caractère," in *Architecture* (Paris, 1788). Also, "Caractère," in *Dictionnaire historique d'architecture* (Paris, 1832).

4 See Wolfgang Herrmann, *The Theory of Claude Perrault* (London, 1962).

5 Charles-Etienne Briseaux, *Traité du beau essentiel dans les arts* (Paris, 1752).

6 See Joseph Rykwert, *The First Moderns* (Cambridge: The MIT Press, 1980), ch. 8.

7 For this and other contemporary opinions about Sainte-Geneviève, see R. D. Middleton, "The Abbé de Cordemoy and the Graeco Gothic Ideal," *Journal of the Warburg and Courtauld Institutes* 25 (1962):111.

8 The search, during the Enlightenment, for the laws of a universal grammar was founded on the work of the Port Royale Grammarians, Arnaud and Lancelot, whose *Grammaire générale et raisonnée* was published in 1660. The English grammarian James Harris (1709–80) defined universal grammar as "that grammar which, without regarding the several idioms of particular languages, only respects those principles that are essential to them all." The principal figures of this tradition were César Chesneau Dumarsais (1676–1746), Nicolas Beauzée (1717–89), and Destutt de Tracy (1754–1836).

9 J.-N.-L. Durand, "Introduction," *Précis des leçons d'architecture données à l'Ecole Royale Polytechnique* (Paris, 1819).

10 Jacques-Guillaume Legrand, *Essai sur l'histoire générale de l'architecture* (Paris, 1800).

11 Thomas Hope, *An Historical Essay on Architecture*, 3rd ed. (1840), vol. 1, p. 495; quoted in D. Watkin, *Thomas Hope and the Neoclassical Idea* (London, 1968), p. 214.

12 The crucial document of romantic artistic doctrine is the review *Das Athenaeum* (1798–1800), written mostly by Friedrich and August Wilhelm Schlegel. This doctrine was disseminated in France and England by Madame de Stäel, whose book *De l'Allemagne* was published in 1813.

13 See Peter Collins, *Changing Ideals in Modern Architecture* (Toronto: McGill University Press, 1967), ch. 19, "Rationalism."

14 Léonce Reynard, *Traité d'architecture* (Paris, 1860–63), p. ix.

15 See Collins, *Changing Ideals*, ch. 19.

16 Viollet-le-Duc's principal theoretical statements are to be found in the *Dictionnaire raisonné d'architecture française, du XIe au XVIe siècle* (Paris, 1858–68) and *Entretiens sur l'architecture* (Paris, 1863–72).

17 Viollet-le-Duc, *Entretiens*, no. 10.

18 See Philippe Junod, "La terminologie esthétique de Viollet-le-Duc," in *Viollet-le-Duc, centenaire de sa mort à Lausanne* (Lausanne, 1979), p. 57.

19   Viollet-le-Duc, "Style," in *Dictionnaire raisonné.*

20   See Junod, "La terminologie."

21   A. W. Schlegel, *Uber Dramatische Kunst and Literatur,* 2nd ed. (Heidelberg, 1817), III, p. 8; cited by Rene Wellek, *A History of Modern Criticism* (Cambridge, 1981), vol. 2, p. 148.

22   Louis Sullivan, *Kindergarten Chats and Other Writings* (New York, 1979), p. 194.

23   The German formalist aesthetic philosophers were antagonistic to the classical theory of imitation. According to Johann Friedrich Herbart (1776–1841), beauty is an irreducible sensation which "means" nothing beyond itself. Herbart's approach was developed in different ways, and in the different arts, by Wilhelm Unger, Robert Zimmermann, Eduard Hanslick, Konrad Fiedler, and others, up to the end of the nineteenth century.

24   Ernst Mach, *Die Mechanik in ihrer Entwicklung.*

25   Bronislaw Malinowski, "Anthropology," in *Encyclopaedia Britannica,* 13th ed., supplement 1 (Chicago, 1926).

26   See Claude Schnaidt, *Hannes Meyer* (Arthur Nigli, 1965), p. 23.

27   See Hermann Muthesius's "Proposition" in the *Proceedings of the Deutscher Werkbund Congress at Cologne* (1914). In 1912 the English critic T. E. Hulme also made an analogy between classicism and the machine when attacking expressionist poetry. See Raymond Williams, *Culture and Society* (New York, 1958).

28   See Ignacio Sola-Morales, "Critical Discipline," *Oppositions* 23 (Winter 1981). This is a sensitive study of the work and ideas of Giorgio Grassi. See also Aldo Rossi, *The Architecture of the City* (Cambridge: The MIT Press, 1982) and *A Scientific Autobiography* (Cambridge: the MIT Press, 1981).

29   Paul Valéry, "Introduction à la méthode de Leonard de Vinci," *La Nouvelle revue française,* August 15, 1895; translated in James R. Lawler, ed., *Paul Valéry, An Anthology* (Princeton: Princeton University Press, 1976), p. 61.

II   **Traditions and Displacements:**
      Three Studies of Le Corbusier

Architecture and Engineering:
Le Corbusier and the Paradox of Reason

In his book *David to Delacroix*,[1] Walter Friedlander distinguishes between two great currents in French painting, which he calls the rational and the irrational. These categories, if we accept them, must apply in some measure to the other arts, including architecture. The rational current is moralizing and didactic, and it belongs to the tradition of French classicism. It is tempting to see Le Corbusier as belonging to this didactic tradition and as bringing to the architectural avant-garde of the 1920s a peculiarly French combination of moralism, formalism, and classicism.[2]

Of all the architects of the modern movement, it is Le Corbusier who constructed its most elaborate theoretical underpinning. His architectural theory differs significantly from that of the other modern architects, in kind as well as degree. Whereas for Walter Gropius theory was *instrumental* and design its direct product, for Le Corbusier theory was *justificatory*. It seeks to justify architecture as an autonomous[3] and normative discipline, and in this way belongs to the tradition of French architectural theory from Philibert de L'Orme to Ledoux. His theoretical writings aimed to reconcile new phenomena resulting from modern industrial production with certain *a priori* architectural values. These values were seen as the conditions that made the practice of architecture intelligible.

Le Corbusier has often been called a positivist and has been criticized for trying to apply to the twentieth century a mental set belonging to the nine-

Originally published in *Modulus* (1980–81).

teenth century. Although he shared with the positivists their epistemological formalism, he did not share the priority they gave to the Fact.[4] As he says in *Vers une architecture*, "Architectural abstraction has the particular and magnificent property that, rooted in the brute fact it spiritualizes it, because the brute fact is nothing but the materialization, the symbol, of the possible Idea."[5]

Le Corbusier's formalism aimed at being theoretically systematic but did not necessarily aim at the transformation of the real world. Yet it is easy to see why Le Corbusier has been called a positivist: he tenaciously clung to final solutions, as if he were asserting a direct, Bentham-like relation between form and function. This quality in Le Corbusier's work can be seen if we compare him with the Russian Constructivist theoreticians, who believed that theoretical systems and action on the material of the real world coincided. For them the empirical could always be used to criticize and modify artistic form, and such modifications would make these forms theoretically *more* correct. For Le Corbusier the empirical inhabits a different world from the ideal; there is never any possibility of a direct passage from Fact to Meaning. When he insisted on the inviolate quality of his designs, he was defending their ideal qualities and not their empirical ones. Indeed, he often clung to design solutions against all empirical evidence, as in the case of the Salvation Army Hostel, whose history has been documented by Brian Brace Taylor.[6]

Le Corbusier's architecture, its qualities as well as what may perhaps be considered its faults, comes directly from this dualistic philosophy. Nonetheless, he never satisfactorily reconciled his search for the timeless human values of architecture with his belief that modern technology and the structures of modern capitalism provided the means whereby these values could be reestablished in a new form.

Le Corbusier's discourse attempted to synthesize, insofar as the problem of architecture was concerned, the contradictory world views current at the time of his intellectual formation. To understand these world views, and their resulting ideologies and contradictions, one must turn back to the architectural discourse of the seventeenth century, the moment when the Vitruvian tradition was first challenged. The form of this challenge is well known. In dividing architectural beauty into two kinds, *certain beauty* and *arbitrary beauty*, Claude Perrault introduced into architectural discourse the epistemological distinction between *a priori* and empirical knowledge, between the natural sign and the arbitrary sign, a distinction paralleled in contemporary philosophy and linguistic theory.[7] Perrault's definition could be interpreted in two ways: either as encouraging the search for natural causes of absolute beauty, which were no longer seen as derived from ancient authority, or as encouraging skepticism.

Perrault's theory exerted an influence on other architects, notably Christopher Wren. From Wren's notes, published in the *Parentalia,* one can see that Perrault's method was often used by subsequent theorists, not to justify custom and association as the basis of the architectural sign, but to find new sources of certainty which were accessible to reason. The empirical method discredited the old *a priori* certainties but created new ones in their place. A new set of phenomena hitherto thought of as secondary, particularly those in the field of optics, was now seen as subject to law and necessity and accessible to experiment and mathematical treatment. This conviction that taste and aesthetic judgment could be shown to rest on natural principles is characteristic of an important strand of eighteenth-century thought. We recognize elements of this view in the thought of Le Corbusier.

By the end of the nineteenth century, however, this view had been modified and distorted by both positivism and historicism, which gave an entirely new emphasis to the problem of the lawlike nature of the world of man's experience: the first, by saying that knowledge finds its verification and ultimate meaning in action on the material world; the second, by trying to reconcile absolute truth with historical change and development. In Le Corbusier's thought these two impulses are overlaid by the idealism prevalent in the late nineteenth century, which was antipositivist and antimaterialist and which somehow accepted the idealism of Hegel without the cultural relativism to which Hegel's system gave rise.[8]

In *The Education of Le Corbusier,*[9] Paul Turner provides evidence that Le Corbusier was strongly influenced by Henry Provensal's book *L'art de Demain*, published in 1907. According to Turner, this book stresses the accessibility of the Hegelian "Idea" to the intuitive grasp of the artist. This "Idea" does not seem identical to eighteenth-century notions which held that truth and beauty are eternal because man is always and everywhere the same. Instead, it seems to assume an emergent Idea, which is capable for the first time of being realized because of the stage of historical development that man has reached. After a period of divergence, art and science had reached a point at which they once again could coalesce and become transparent to each other. Significantly, this philosophy is based on a certain notion of abstraction. Ideal beauty expressed mind and spirit rather than physical senses. Thus it is linked with science. Provensal's contention was that "Science, which begins by enfeebling sentiment, ends by strengthening it."[10]

This quality of abstraction has two interesting corollaries. First, architecture and music are considered the highest of the arts because both "resort to abstractions." (The idea of music as the paradigm for the arts was of course common at the end of the nineteenth century.) Second, architecture is said to be concerned with cubic form, expressing directly the forms of mineral crystals which, alone among natural forms, are said to reveal nature's underlying mathematical structure. Architecture, says Provensal, is a matter of the composition of volumes, the juxtaposition of solid and void, of shade and light. "The artist," he says, "will find the elements of realization of material where the plastic drama is crystallized under the beneficient action of light." Turner points out the obvious parallel between this and Le Corbusier's well-known formulation of architecture as "the learned, correct and magnificent play of volumes assembled in light."[11]

Turner's analysis of Provensal's text helps to solve a problem. Through it we are able to connect two ideas that have always seemed contradictory in Le Corbusier's thought: the idea of absolute and unchanging artistic values associated with eighteenth-century classicism, and the idea of the spirit of the age, which stems from Hegel and the German historicist tradition. In Provensal's book, we find the combination of absolute values and the avant-garde idea of the "new." Hegel's grand cycle seems to have come to an end; the Spirit stands finally exposed, and once it has been revealed by an artistic elite, it will become accessible to all. This cyclical view of history, which invokes the idea of a return or repetition, is put forward explicitly by Le Corbusier in *Urbanisme*, when he discusses the ages of man.

Provensal's book no doubt helped form certain permanent traits of Le Corbusier's thought concerning the eternal and geometric nature of architecture, its relation to science at a fundamental level, and the idea of an imminent discovery, of an apocalyptic moment. Many other experiences, however, helped to crystallize Le Corbusier's conception of a new architecture, three of which seem to be of special importance. The first was the regionalist and artisanal doctrine Le Corbusier absorbed from his teacher at La Chaux-de-Fonds, L'Eplattenier.[12] This doctrine was derived from the Arts and Crafts movement and Owen Jones's theories of ornament. L'Eplattenier taught that nature could be reduced to an underlying geometric structure. This notion was in many ways the antithesis of Provensal's ideas, since, instead of postulating an abstract Idea which could be represented directly, it saw the Idea as something revealed or disclosed in the concrete conditions of a particular time and place. It was part of a tradition that thought in terms of contingent rather than universal meaning and looked for a renewal of architecture through ornament and craftwork.

Le Corbusier was often tempted in his twenties by his vision of an artistic élite creating a popular art out of local conditions. But, at the same time, he was moving away from this vision, toward a more universalist view. Even when he traveled to Turkey and became absorbed in folk architecture, what most intrigued him was the way it could be reduced to a typology and seen as the basis

Le Corbusier, Villa Fallet in La Chaux-de-Fonds,
1905–6

Le Corbusier, Istanbul, Turkey, travel sketch

of a universal language. Writing later in *Urbanisme,* on the problem of architectural detail, he said:

In the traditional architectural cities one finds habits of construction. Until the 19th century, a window, a door, were "human" holes, elements to the human scale: the roofs were built according to procedures uniformly accepted and excellent. In Istanbul all houses were of wood, all roofs were of the same slope and the same tiles. All religious buildings were of stone.[13]

These traditional qualities are seen as embodying the principles with which to generate an entirely new architecture. There is also here, however, an element of nostalgia, and Le Corbusier never entirely abandoned the notion of an architecture incorporating craft techniques. In the 1930s, he was already combining such elements with the abstract forms of technology, much to the disapproval of the *neue Sachlichkeit* purists.

The second experience was that of the architectural tradition. Among the protagonists of the modern movement a moralistic iconoclasm made it impossible to speak of tradition in any but the most general terms. To some extent Le Corbusier shared this attitude. But, sweeping as many of his judgments about architectural history were, they were nonetheless based on a close study of buildings and texts. For him, the tradition which had to be preserved and transformed was more than a set of moral precepts. It was, above all, a set of concrete examples, and the way he communicated this knowledge was by drawing.

Most of Le Corbusier's general precepts seem to have their origin in particular examples: Turkish houses, the monasteries of Mount Athos and Emo, the temple sites of India, Cambodia, and Chaldaea, Pompeian houses, the urban schemes of Louis XIV, the studios and cafes of late-nineteenth-century Paris. This habit of mind is not restricted to his interest in historical types, but marks his confrontation with the products of modern technology, the *objets-types* of modern civilization. It is an essentially iconic procedure. The "Idea" is approached through the image. His mental wardrobe is full of objects ready to be used in a *bricolage*—objects which seem each been imprinted on his memory in a moment of epiphany.

Of the influences mentioned so far, that of Provensal and L'Eplattenier were concerned with theoretical principles. The final influence to be mentioned is the constructive principle exemplified in modern building technology. The sources of this influence lay outside the immediate experience of La Chaux-de-Fonds, in the industrially advanced countries, especially Germany and France.

We have seen that, to some extent, the Hegelian idealism associated with Provensal's theories and the regionalism associated with L'Eplattenier were antagonistic to each other. It is also obvious that modern industry and technology

Le Corbusier, Maison de Mme. de Mandrot, 1930–31

were antagonistic to the revival of the crafts. Modern construction and the idealism of pure form both presuppose abstraction. Yet the abstraction of pure geometry differs from that of modern production techniques because the latter are concerned with the real, empirical world. Such an abstraction is the inheritor of nineteenth-century positivism and instrumentalism, and to this extent is incompatible with the notion of ideal and absolute standards of beauty.

When Le Corbusier went to Germany, he was faced with modes of operation and a scale of production that were both abstract and instrumental. He admired the work of Behrens for AEG, and he found Muthesius's ideas sympathetic, insofar as they gave priority to spiritual over material values. (Muthesius had said that engineering buildings have aesthetic value *if* they embody formal principles, not *because* they embody these principles.[14]) But the utilitarian and materialistic nature of German culture did not seem to Le Corbusier to reflect this idea.[15]

Le Corbusier's response to Paris was different. In the principles of reinforced concrete developed by Auguste Perret he seems to have found an interpretation of constructional rationalism that was compatible with his idealism. One reason for this was the plastic nature of concrete and its malleability to the will of the designer. But in spite of the syntheses of classicism à la Behrens and Perret's rationalism that he achieved in the Villa Schwob, Le Corbusier was evidently still acutely aware of the conflict between an aesthetic idealism leaning toward the classical and an avant-gardism that wished to embrace the most modern tendencies. This conflict forms the subject of several extended passages in both *Vers une architecture* and *Urbanisme,* and they are worth analyzing in some detail.

The first fundamental idea put forward in *Vers une architecture* is that by committing himself to the general principles of modern engineering, the architect will rediscover the sources of his own discipline. To demonstrate this Le Corbusier must first distinguish between engineering and architecture. The aim of the engineer is to provide what is *useful.* The aim of the architect is to *arouse emotion.* But since the engineer, through calculation, produces forms in harmony with the universe, and since the highest form of emotion aroused by architecture comes from its conformity with the selfsame universal laws, it follows that the engineer and the architect share a common foundation.[16] In this theory the difference between the engineer and the architect seems to lie in the degree of intentionality. Engineers make architecture, as it were, unintentionally. They make us feel harmony, but it is in the intentional manipulation of his feeling of harmony that the work of the architect lies. Thus, if in one sense the engineer and the architect start from the same foundation, in another sense architecture has its own basis, which lies in its ability to strike our senses by means of clear, simple forms. The engineer, proceeding by the route of knowl-

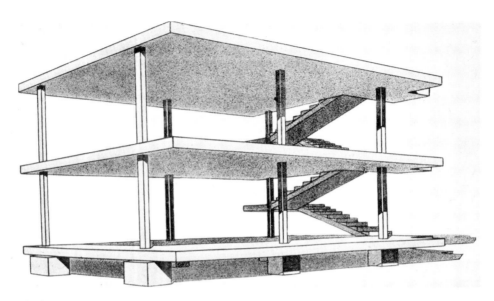

Le Corbusier, Maison Dom-ino prototype, 1914

edge, merely shows us the path of truth, whereas the architect makes this truth palpable.

This truth of the architect does not rest at brutal and obvious sensations. "Certain relations," Le Corbusier says, "are born which agitate our consciousness and put us in a state of joy (*jouissance*), when man makes use of memory, of examination, of reasoning, of creation.[17] By this statement Le Corbusier opens up architecture to an incalculable and infinite "culture." By implication, all the traditional values of architecture are invoked (since memory is involved).

But immediately, and without transition, he counters this idea by saying that our external world has been transformed as a result of the machine and that we have a new vision and a new social life.[18] We seem to see here an implied distinction between an internal, spiritual world that somehow remains constant in the face of an external world that has been completely transformed.

The dichotomy between engineering and architecture is taken up again in a later chapter. Here he says that when a thing responds to a need it satisfies "the whole of the first part of our mind"—that part in which the ultimate satisfaction of the spirit is not possible. This satisfaction belongs to architecture, through its attainment of "a state of Platonic grandeur, mathematical order, speculation, and the perception of harmony, through relationships which are moving."[19] The status of the useful in this *architectural* purpose is not made clear. One is left to deduce that concentration on the useful and the necessary purges the mind and frees it for Platonic contemplation. There is thus a moral imperative, an imperative of self-denial and asceticism, which seems to be the condition of aesthetic pleasure.

In discussing the aesthetic, Le Corbusier divides it into the sensuous and the intellectual. The sensuous is that aspect always enjoyed by simple peoples, and is expressed in decoration and color. The intellectual is that aspect enjoyed by cultivated peoples, and is expressed in harmony and proportion. Each aspect is defined as "necessary superfluity."[20] But, immediately after this, he says that utility and economy provide satisfaction to the mind, whereas form (cubes, cylinders, etc.) provides satisfaction to the senses.[21] We therefore have a schema in which proportion and harmony belong to the *mind* in relation to decoration, but to the *senses* in relation to utility. The attribution of intellectual satisfaction to utility *and* to aesthetic form seems to suggest that he interprets "intellect" (*esprit*) in two diametrically opposed ways, one deriving from rationalism or positivism, the other from neoplatonism.

In *Urbanisme* the theme of the engineer and the architect, reason and sentiment, is treated with greater breadth and at a more philosophical level. First Le Corbusier propounds a theory of cultural evolution, based on general eighteenth-century models from Rousseau to Hegel and resembling that of Vico in its cyclical implications. According to this scheme, the history of culture consists of three stages: that of the "human Animal," that of "the road to culture," and that of "the achievement of Equilibrium." In the first phase, man acts instinctively in accordance with universal law; in the second, acquisition of knowledge throws him into disequilibrium and awareness of his ignorance; and in the third, there is a new fusion of knowledge and universal law.[22]

The third stage is identified with classicism, in which, Le Corbusier says, we create "coldly and purely." Geometry and the right angle are the emblems of this stage. "The purpose of art," says Le Corbusier, "is to raise us above disorder and by this means to give us the spectacle of equilibrium."[23] There are three classical moments—Greece and Rome, the eighteenth century, and the modern world. Between these moments come periods of preparation, the Middle Ages and the nineteenth century, in which the acquisition of new knowledge throws the previous system into disequilibrium, but at the same time presages a new state of harmony.

Le Corbusier then discusses the role of intuition and sentiment (the sphere of the artist) within this cycle.[24] "Intuition," he says, "is the sum of acquired knowledge," which has been inscribed in the collective memory. "Sentiment" is an "emanation" of this inscribed knowledge. Thus, intuition and sentiment are not antagonistic to reason. They are, rather, reason under its instinctive, sensuous, and emotive aspects. Since, in the first instance, sentiment is dependent on reason, it is something that is "earned." It cannot be enjoyed cheaply, "it cannot be 'stolen'." This earned sentiment leads us beyond everyday experiences toward ideal form, toward style, toward culture. A sort of pyramid is implied, with pragmatic reason at the base and the concept of ideal form at the apex.

We have now, says Le Corbusier, arrived at the fateful moment in the historical cycle when our sentimental urges must be seen as identical to the rule of reason. The general, the typical, and the common appeal to us more than the individual and the exceptional. Sentiment no longer strives to be heroic: it recognizes that the truly heroic is found in the apparently banal world of facts, disclosed by science.[25] This is true because the means at our disposal are now completely adequate to the ends desired. The state of equilibrium and calm thus attained are to be described as classical and are shared by all classical ages.

But at the same time, because we are wedded to outworn patterns of thought and response, this involves the complete upheaval of accepted ideas and the creation of something new.[26] Now, according to Le Corbusier's own reasoning, one would expect this situation of newness to produce a state of anxiety and strain; and one would expect classical equilibrium to be the outcome of gradual cultural acclimatization. But this obvious contradiction is elided in Le Corbusier's text. Instead, in the manner of Provensal's theory, the classical-eternal and the messianic-revolutionary are conflated.

Le Corbusier now looks at the conflict between the engineer and the architect from another angle. It is the nature of practical engineering to produce results that are provisional, whereas the work of art has a value that is perennial.[27]

Modern industrialism is the result of abstract reasoning, not of passion. It has no more need for "great men," only for "little men" with limited aims. "The work of reason," he says,

is cumulative and adds to itself little by little. . . . In our passions we are like a wine which is exported: we do not know at which table it will be served. The great works of humanity are elaborated more and more audaciously, and with a temerity which could bring down on us the anger of the gods.[28]

He adds:

The poet, on the other hand, judges and discerns the lasting quality of words. He is at the opposite pole from the calculators, and he follows the undulating curve of the passions. Beyond the utilitarian he discerns the imperishable—man.[29]

But for Le Corbusier, this simple opposition between the man of science and the poet is very deceptive.[30] For if it is true that when we look at the world of the engineer we see a "mêlée of mediocre destinies," we also see "the rigor of works which move in a perfectly regulated way toward imposing realizations":

Until now, the artifact was so precarious, so far from perfection, that it could not attract attention to the detriment of passion. . . . [But] a great revolution has intervened . . . which has overturned our equilibrium. . . . Suddenly we are armed with a fabulous apparatus which upsets our admirations and compromises our age-old hierarchies. . . . Reason? Passion? Two currents, two individuals who oppose one another. One looks behind, one ahead; one poet shines over the ruins, but the other may well be exterminated.[31]

The poet, therefore, must accept and celebrate the end products of that "man of mediocre destiny," the engineer.

But Le Corbusier still has doubts. If mechanical beauty were the result of pure reason, it would be perishable. In mechanical work, the most recent work is always the most beautiful. "Thus, beauty would be ephemeral and would soon fall into ridicule."[32] He asks himself whether the emotion produced by Eiffel's Gabarit bridge will persist. "Here," he says, "reason does not suffice, and one has to suspend judgment. Here we see the mystery that surrounds the future of contemporary individual works. . . . When the passion of a man has passed, the works will continue to exist."[33] In other words, the work may survive its power to give rise to sensations of beauty and prove itself, *in retrospect*, to be lacking in those timeless qualities that constitute the true work of architecture.

Gustave Eiffel, Gabarit Bridge

Le Corbusier replies to this objection with a counter argument. It would, he says, be a dangerous verdict if (realizing this fact) we were to expect the engineer to put himself at the service of the man of passion; he would lose his *raison d'être*. Quite the contrary, it is the man of passion who must give way to the engineer:

Individual passion only has the right to incarnate the collective phenomenon. The collective phenomenon is the state of soul of an epoch, conditioned in general as it is in the particular. . . . A general state of thinking is established . . . and the works of calculation . . . are carried by the general passion and enter into the measure of man. . . . In front of the works of calculation one is face to face with a phenomenon of high poetry; the individual is not responsible for it. . . . Man realizes his potential.[34]

Here we see Le Corbusier resorting to the Hegelian world-spirit. Only if we attribute a kind of human will to this spirit do the words "passion," "sentiment," and "beauty" still have meaning.[35] But Le Corbusier does not explain how we are to reconcile this with the continued existence of the architect. If followed to its logical conclusion it would result in the disappearance of artistic production altogether. The artist-architect would no longer be needed for the task of idealization. This task would be carried out unintentionally by the engineer, as the stand-in or proxy for the world-spirit. The ideological formation characteristic of the artist would be a thing of the past. At best, the artist-architect would become a sort of voyeur, passively echoing the dictates of history and abstract reason. Utopia would circulate continuously and weightlessly within reality.

But there is another idea suggested by this new interpretation of the artist. This is the Hegelian notion that the poet/philosopher is able to grasp the whole of history and see in it the operation of reason. This could be called the "overview" theory. It has implications for space as well as time. The pattern which the industrial order imprints on the earth, while fragmentary and alienating at ground level, can be seen to be meaningful from a sufficiently high altitude. The airplane is obviously a powerful symbol of this notion of overview, and it is not surprising that Le Corbusier talks so much about the view of buildings from the air.

Having considered the main problem dealt with in Le Corbusier's theory, one must now look at aspects of his theory covering the two specific areas of concern in his first works: urbanism and buildings. Although Le Corbusier's refusal to make any distinctions between architecture and town planning is theoretically correct, the difference in his application of theory to each field is so great that it seems legitimate to revert to the conventional distinction when considering the relation of his theory to his practice.

When Le Corbusier applies his theory to the city, he simply reverts to the unresolved duality between the engineer and the architect. The architect re-emerges in his pure ideological role. "The city," he says,

is profoundly anchored in the regions of calculation. . . . This will be essential for what is useful, and in consequence, perishable. . . . It remains for the city to last, for which other things than calculation are needed. This will be architecture, which is all that is beyond calculation.[36]

This simple dichotomy results in the setting side by side of the products of pragmatic reasoning and the establishment of pure form. The logic of the engineer results in the clear separation of functions, the total subjection of urban man to a process of abstract classification. In this way the Corbusian city is a kind of diagrammatic representation of the properties of the modern city as described by the nineteenth-century German sociologist Georg Simmel. According to Simmel, all relations in the modern city are abstract and are reduced to quantity. The paradigm of this abstraction is money, the means by which the qualitative difference between objects is reduced to pure quantity.[37]

The abstract sociological implications of the Corbusian city are translated directly into their plastic equivalent—abstract geometrical form. Both on a sociological and an aesthetic level, there is a distance set up between everyday concrete existence and gratification. At the level of aesthetic response this distance is expressed in great ensembles seen in light.

This abstract and "inhuman" aspect of the Corbusian city has often been remarked on. But we should remember Le Corbusier's own explanation of it. He saw it as an ideal, theoretical demonstration, not the plan for a real city.

Writing of the Ville Contemporaine in *Urbanisme*, he says:

Proceeding in the manner of an experimenter in his laboratory . . . I excluded all accidents, I gave myself an ideal terrain. The object was not to overcome the conditions of the preexistent city, but to construct a theoretically watertight system, *to formulate the fundamental principles of modern urbanism. These principles,* if they are not contradicted, *can form the skeleton of the contemporary system of urbanism; they are the rule according to which the game can be played. After this, one looks at the special case—that is to say any case whatever—: Paris, London, New York, or some small provincial town.*[38] [my emphasis]

Similarly, describing the Plan Voisin for Paris, he says, "The plan does not claim to have found the final solution to the problems of the center of Paris, but it may serve to raise the discussion to a level in keeping with the spirit of our age."[39] These disclaimers might be indicative of a certain skepticism. Although the logic is impeccable, he seems to say, the premise on which it is based might conceivably be contradicted, just as a scientific hypothesis can be refuted.

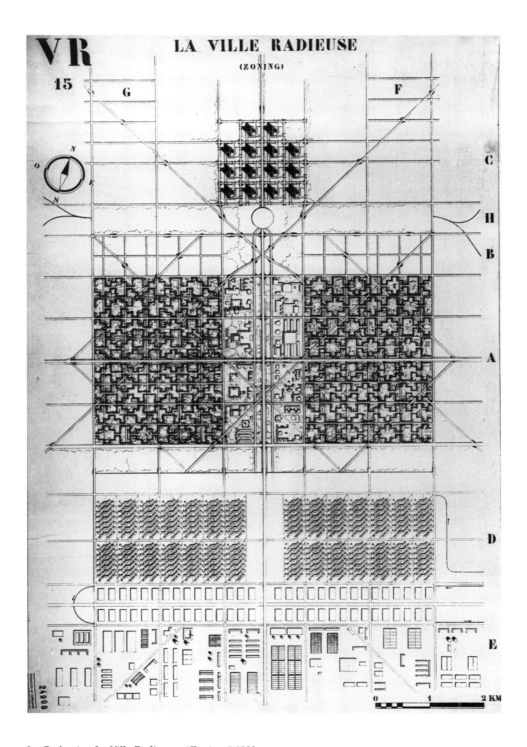

105

Le Corbusier, La Ville Radieuse, "Zoning," 1933

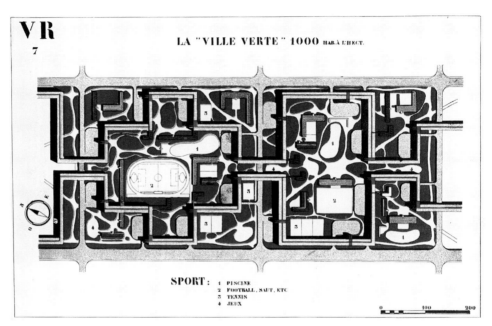

106

Le Corbusier, La Ville Verte for 1000 Inhabitants,
"Sport," 1933

On the other hand, Le Corbusier's city is anything but a model in the scientific sense. It is a concrete image, fully worked out in all its details. Therefore one is forced to question the status of the general principles that the city illustrates. Is it scientific, neutral, and refutable, or is it artistic, ideological, and apodictic? Everything points to the latter interpretation. But if any further proof were needed, we might notice how Le Corbusier's concept of the city is firmly based on eighteenth-century tradition.

Le Corbusier's connection with eighteenth-century ideas and the way he differs from these is shown in the famous quotation from the Abbé Laugier which says that the city should display uniformity in the detail and a certain chaos in the whole. It is worthwhile to see what Laugier actually says about the city. His opening remarks are:

Most of our towns remain in a state of neglect, of confusion and disorder. . . . One builds new houses, but one does not change the bad distribution of streets. . . . Our towns are what they have been, a mass of houses put together without system, without economy, without design.[40]

This could almost be Le Corbusier speaking—Le Corbusier the rationalist, equating the efficient economic organization of the city with its architectural order. But, curiously enough, it is Laugier's more purely aesthetic doctrine that Le Corbusier is interested in, although he seems to misinterpret it. What is Laugier's aesthetic doctrine? He says the city can be thought of as a forest or a park, where one finds

at the same time, order and bizarrerie, symmetry and variety; . . . here a star, there a patte-d'oie; *on one side spurs, on the other fans; further off parallels; everywhere open spaces of a different figure and design. The more choice, abundance, contrast, disorder in this composition, the more the park will have piquant and delicious beauties. . . . A park that was nothing but an assemblage of isolated and uniform squares, whose routes were only differentiated by number, would be very tedious and flat. In all things let us avoid an excess of regularity and symmetry. . . . Anyone who does not succeed in varying our pleasures never succeeds in pleasing us.*

In a town the magnificence of the whole should be divided into

an infinity of beauties all of different details, where one hardly meets the same objects; where, walking from one end to the other, one finds in each quarter something new . . . where there is order but nonetheless a great confusion; where everything is an alignment but without monotony, and where, from a multitude of regular parts, there results in the whole a certain idea of irregularity and chaos.[41]

Laugier presupposes classical order, regularity, alignment, and magnificence of form. His disorder is seen as a picturesque critique of this; it consists chiefly of the element of surprise. It is a matter of a "multitude of regular parts," that is to say, streets, squares, *pattes-d'oie,* stars, each of which is regular in itself, but all of which are different. Variety is created by using a wide repertoire of conventional urban forms.

Le Corbusier, on the contrary, conflates the notion of chaos, not with surprise, but with magnificence of effect, in blocks *à redents* composed to create plastic movement. Once the pattern is established, it is merely repeated.

At the same time, uniformity in the detail is given a different interpretation. It is not, as it seems to be in Laugier, a question of giving a number of set pieces their own regularity. It is a question of creating a modular repetition of parts, in an attempt to recreate the linguistic order which he had noted in Istanbul, so that the eye will not be distracted from measuring the quality of the whole.[42]

For Laugier's city of surprises to work, one must presuppose a dense tissue, as in the metaphorical hunting forest which the city resembles. But in Le Corbusier there is no tissue, no foreground. Instead, there is a literal forest or park across which one sees, at a distance, the great forms of housing blocks or office blocks. Is this distance not identical with the "overview" previously mentioned?

For Laugier the eighteenth-century city is essentially undesignable. It consists of fragments of order. The mental idea of order no longer has its exact spatial equivalent, as it had in the Renaissance.[43] For Le Corbusier the capitalist city of the twentieth century is completely designable. But in designing it, he succeeds only in showing its monstrosity. There is no way in which the distance between the concrete and the abstract can be abridged. The Corbusian city remains as he saw it: "a theoretically rigorous system," a skeleton on which there is no flesh— and this in spite of its artistic manipulation—so different from the city of Hilberseimer.

Le Corbusier's achievement lies rather in his creation of the fragments of the city. The only scale at which the concrete and the abstract can be reconnected is that of the individual building. If the dualism in Le Corbusier's thought produces an unresolved contradiction in his theory and a disembodied abstraction in his city, then in his buildings this dualism produces a dialectic in which aesthetic meaning is created. This dialectic consists of the interaction of pragmatic order (function) and ideal order (pure form).

Le Corbusier's theory now becomes a set of design principles, the most important of which are contained in the division of the building into volume, surface, and plan[44] and in his "Five Points of a New Architecture.[45]

In the notions of volume, surface, and plan the dialectical process is stated most clearly. Volume, the creation of pure geometric solids, is the fundamental basis of architectural aesthetics. But we do not arrive at architecture, properly speaking, until this volume is penetrated and subdivided by elements of util-

Illustrations of three of Le Corbusier's "Five Points of a New Architecture": *pilotis*, roof gardens, and the free plan

Jusqu'au béton armé et au fer, pour bâtir une maison de pierre, on creusait de larges rigoles dans la terre et l'on allait chercher le bon sol pour établir la fondation.

On constituait ainsi les caves, locaux médiocres, humides généralement.

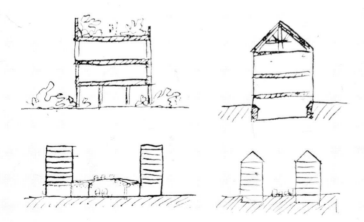

Puis on montait les murs de pierre. On établissait un premier plancher posé sur les murs, puis un second, un troisième; on ouvrait des fenêtres.

Avec le béton armé on supprime entièrement les murs. On porte les planchers sur de minces poteaux disposés à de grandes distances les uns des autres.

ity—specifically, with openings. These appear, phenomenally, as elements on the surface of the volume. The subdivisions, penetrations, etc. of this surface can either reinforce the basic volumes or destroy them. It is the architect's task to reinforce them.[46]

The plan is the means by which the three-dimensional volume is established. It seems, though Le Corbusier nowhere says this, that in spite of rigorously diagrammatic qualities, the plan will reflect the three-dimensional form of the building. Since it is an iconic sign (in the Peircian sense) of the building, it will have strong iconic properties of its own. This is always true of Le Corbusier's plans. The same dialectic is present in the plan as in the building as a whole. Thus, while the ideal order of the building implies a symmetrical and axial organization of the plan and all its parts, utility demands that this ideal order be modified. Le Corbusier gives a paradigmatic example in the House of the Tragic Poet in Pompeii. He says of this plan:

Everything is on axis but you cannot pass in a straight line. The axis is in the intentions, and the dignity given by the axis extends to humble things which the axis accommodates itself to. You get the impression that everything is ordered, but the sensation is rich. You notice then the comfortable breaking of the axis, which gives intensity to the volumes.[47]

Here it is clear that the pragmatic and utilitarian needs do not for Le Corbusier weaken the aesthetic meaning, but make it richer and more complex. We see therefore that Le Corbusier's ideas of both surface and plan reflect the same principles: a primary formal law brought into collision with utility, such that both interact within the complex whole of the work of architecture—a whole that includes both order and disorder.

The Five Points of a new architecture reinterpret the traditional elements of architecture in terms of this dialectic. First, the plan and the internal volumes are freed from the constraints of structure to take on configurations demanded by utility and convenience. At the same time, this freedom allows these volumes to take on anthropomorphic significance by means of visual metaphors in a way which is closely related to the objects represented in Purist paintings.[48] Third, the building is raised on *pilotis* and has a flat roof, and the facade (the surface) is projected forward from the structure. Any of these three moves helps to give the total volume maximum isolation and purity.

There is a further consequence of the projection of the surface from the structure: the surface becomes a thin membrane—a *pure surface.* Indentations of this surface become explosive, since there is no inherent tendency of the surface itself to become modulated in any way (as for instance a masonry wall with pilasters or buttresses). These penetrations enable sculptural and anthropomorphic internal elements to be sensed simultaneously with the surface. Meaning (given by the elements derived from human life) and pure form exist in a

House of the Tragic Poet, sketch of plan by Le
Corbusier, 1911

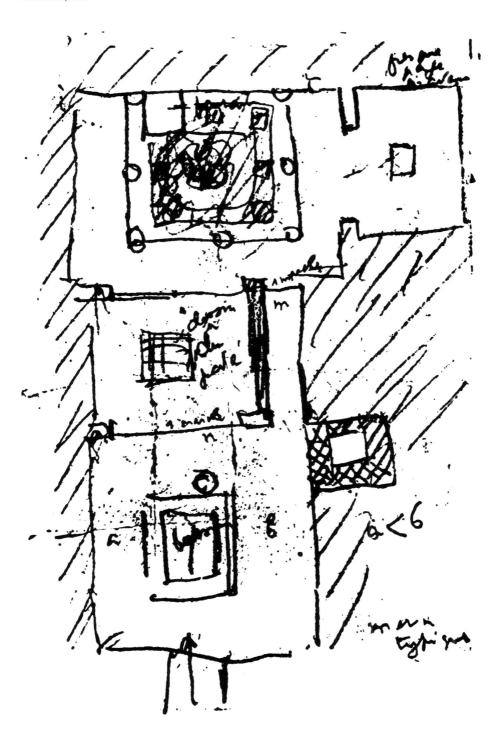

Le Corbusier, Villa Savoye, 1929–31, architectural promenade

Le Corbusier, Villa Savoye, facade

114

Le Corbusier, Villa Savoye, entry hall ramps

state of constant interaction. This is seen in the attic opening in the center of the entrance facade at Garches, where what is discreetly "revealed" is both plastic and asymmetrical, anthropormorphic and chaotic.

The clearest demonstration of this aesthetic system is given by Le Corbusier in his diagrams showing the "Four Compositions." The first, Maison La Roche-Jeanneret, differs from the other three in not being *"le prisme pure."* It can be given order, Le Corbusier says, by classification and hierarchy. We can see this as being absorbed into any of the other three compositions.

Of the three pure prisms, the first represents the Villa Stein-de Monzie at Garches.[49] The second, the house in Tunis, is stated as being *"trés facile."* The cube is only suggested by the exposed Dom-ino-like frame, and the free volumes of the interior are generated from the center and move toward the perimeter. In the third, Poissy, which clearly has paradigmatic value for Le Corbusier, the interior volumes are generated from the periphery and move toward the center. The ideal cube is established, but the interior volumes are eaten away.

This brief analysis has only touched on Le Corbusier's architectural "language" and has been restricted to a small body of early work, the period of *L'Esprit Nouveau* and Purism. Nonetheless, it has perhaps shown how his language and his theory were related. The aim has been to reveal some of the ideological roots of Le Corbusier's theory, the contradictions which arose from these, and some of the ways in which the theory was transformed into artistic practice, rather than to establish any fundamentally new thesis about Le Corbusier. Even so, we could generalize by saying that his theory and his practice were attempts to reconcile the traditions of rationalism and idealism, and that his theory is the culmination of a long dispute in which empirical science has progressively challenged the established claims of architecture.

In this historical process the problem of architecture is part of a larger problem involving the whole notion of art. And if Le Corbusier seems to have been more successful in reconciling these contradictory claims in his buildings than in either his theory or his urban projects, it is probably because we can interpret these buildings as belonging to a modernist movement in the arts in general— a movement in which the work of art becomes increasingly solipsistic and self-referential.

Rather than trying to see Le Corbusier's buildings as an attempt to transform the real world, it seems more fruitful to see them as constituting a reflexive system of order, in which contradictions are resolved at the level of metaphor. Whereas in his theory and in his urban projects the contradictions remain in the form of logical antithesis, in his buildings these contradictions interact. As in poetic metaphor, the elements of contradiction are resolved without losing their independence.

Le Corbusier, Villa Stein-de Monzie at Garches,
1927

Le Corbusier, "Four Compositions," 1929

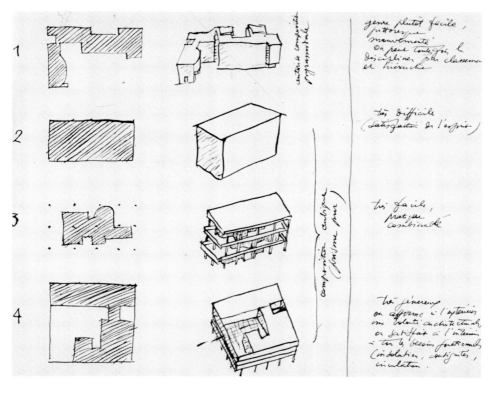

Notes

1 Walter Friedlander, *David to Delacroix*, trans. Robert Goldwater (New York: Schocken Books, 1968).

2 Certain English art historians have recently attacked modernism in architecture because of its concern for morality; see, for example, David Watkin, *Morality and Architecture*. But they ignore the fact that the interaction of moral ideas with the idea of beauty is a characteristic of French classicism (and indeed also of medieval and neoplatonic aesthetics) and is by no means restricted to modern architecture. This interaction is, in fact, inseparable from any aesthetic theory that takes the tradition of rhetoric into account.

3 The word "autonomous" is not used here to imply a discipline divorced from contextual "reality," but rather a discipline that constitutes a specific technique by which this "reality" is transformed.

4 By "formalism" I mean the idea that the logical and formal properties of the mind correspond in some way to the "real" world. This can take a materialist or an idealist form, depending on whether priority is given to things or to ideas.

5 Le Corbusier, *Vers une architecture* (Paris: Editions Crès, 1923), p. 15.

6 Brian Brace Taylor, *La Cité de Refuge di Le Corbusier 1929–1933* (Rome: Officina Edizione, 1979).

7 See Wolfgang Herrmann, *The Theory of Claude Perrault* (London: A. Zwemmer, 1973).

8 The influence of Hegelian idealism, or some popular version of it, on the avant-garde of the early twentieth century is noted by Christopher Gray, *Cubist Aesthetic Theories* (Baltimore: Johns Hopkins Press, 1953).

9 Paul Venable Turner, *The Education of Le Corbusier* (New York and London: Garland Publishing, Inc., 1977). The first part of this essay is much indebted to Turner's study.

10 Ibid., p. 18.

11 Ibid., pp. 21–22.

12 See Stanislaus von Moos, *Le Corbusier: Elements of a Synthesis* (Cambridge: The MIT Press, 1979), p. 2.

13 Le Corbusier, *Urbanisme* (Paris: Editions Crès, 1924), p. 66.

14 Turner, *Education*, p. 77.

15 Ibid., p. 76. Jeanneret's *Etude sur le mouvement d'art décoratif en Allemagne*, however, shows that he was considerably more enthusiastic about German artistic developments when he visited that country in 1910 than the anti-German tone of his later writings would lead one to believe. Moreover, it is clear that many of the key concepts in the *L'Esprit Nouveau* articles—including the distinction between architecture and engineering—owe their inception to the Deutscher Werkbund, whose third annual conference in Berlin he attended.

See Winifred Nerdinger, "Standard et Type: Le Corbusier et Allemagne 1920–1927," in *L'Esprit Nouveau: Le Corbusier et Industrie 1920–1925*, ed. Stanislaus von

Moos (Strasbourg: Les Musées de la ville de Strasbourg, 1987); and Werner Oechslin, "Influences, confluences et reniements," in *Le Corbusier: Une Encyclopedie*, ed. Jacques Lucan (Paris: Centre Georges Pompidou, 1987).

16 Le Corbusier, *Vers une architecture*, p. 7.

17 Ibid., p. 8.

18 Ibid.

19 Ibid., p. 87.

20 Ibid., p. 114.

21 Ibid.

22 Le Corbusier, *Urbanisme*, p. 34.

23 Ibid., p. 35.

24 Ibid., p. 33.

25 Ibid., p. 37.

26 Ibid.

27 Ibid., p. 46.

28 Ibid., p. 44.

29 Ibid.

30 Ibid.

31 Ibid., p. 45.

32 Ibid., p. 46.

33 Ibid., p. 48.

34 Ibid., p. 49.

35 The finality that Le Corbusier attributes to technology is an extension of the Hegelian notion by which, as Lucio Colletti says, "material and effective causality . . . becomes a moment within ideal causality, i.e. within finalism or teleology." See Lucio Colletti, *Marxism and Hegel* (London, 1973), p. 210.

36 Le Corbusier, *Urbanisme*, p. 50.

37 See Georg Simmel, "Die Grosstädte und das Geistesleben" (1903) trans. Kurt H. Wolff, *The Sociology of Georg Simmel* (Glencoe, Ill.: The Free Press of Glencoe, Illinois, 1950).

38 Le Corbusier, *Urbanisme*, p. 158.

39 Ibid., p. 273.

40 P. Laugier, *Essai sur l'architecture* (Paris, 1753). The actual quotation used by Le Corbusier comes in Laugier's later essay, *Observations sur l'architecture* (The Hague, 1765).

41 Ibid.

42 Le Corbusier, *Urbanisme*, p. 67.

43 Pierre Patte's plan of Paris, in which he plots the results of a competition for monuments to Louis XV, may perhaps give some idea of Laugier's concept. Admittedly, this a "composite" plan, but the very idea of superimposing different fragments on the same plan is suggestive of Laugier's picturesque model. According to Herrmann (*Laugier and 18th Century French Theory*, London, 1961), Patte acknowledged his general indebtedness to Laugier.

44 Le Corbusier, *Vers une architecture*, "les trois Rappels."

45 Le Corbusier, *Oeuvre complète 1910–1929*, vol. 1 (Zurich: Editions d'Architecture, 1964).

46 Le Corbusier, *Vers une architecture*, p. 25.

47 Ibid., p. 153.

48 For an interesting discussion of the anthropomorphism in Le Corbusier's free-form volumes in relation to the abstract space of the grid, see Kurt Forster, "Antiquity and Modernity in the La Roche-Jeanneret Houses of 1923," *Oppositions* 15/16 (1980): 131–53.

49 See Le Corbusier, *Précisions* (Paris: Edition Vincent Freal and Cie, 1960).

The Strategies of the *Grands Travaux*

$\mathbf{A}$mong the illustrations of the Centrosoyus and the Cité de Refuge in Le Corbusier's *Oeuvre complète* are two showing the projects extended to adjacent sites to form complexes that assume the scale and texture of urban fragments. The Centrosoyus extension visualizes a new administrative district with the Centrosoyus building as an organic part.[1] The extension of the Cité de Refuge proposes a Cité d'Hospitalisation linked to a new wing of the original building.

At first sight there is nothing particularly surprising in these extensions, given Le Corbusier's tendency to treat each of his projects not only as the solution to a particular set of problems, but also as a prototypical element in a new urban totality. Yet the more we look at them, the more problematic they become. First, in being dissolved into general urban texture and in thus losing their uniqueness, they seem to suffer a loss of representational power. Second, though the urban continuum they imply bears an obvious resemblance to such urban projects as the plan for the Porte de Sainte-Cloud of 1938, this resemblance seems purely formal.

Whether we interpret these two projects as administrative buildings or as "social condensers" on the model of the Soviet avant-garde, it is difficult to imagine them constituting part of the linear continuum Le Corbusier reserved exclusively for housing in all his city plans. These extensions force a reinterpretation of the buildings according to which they become hybrids, hovering uncertainly

Originally published in *Le Corbusier: une Encyclopédie,* ed. Jacques Lucan (Paris: Centre Georges Pompidou, 1987). First published in English in *Assemblage* 4 (October 1987).

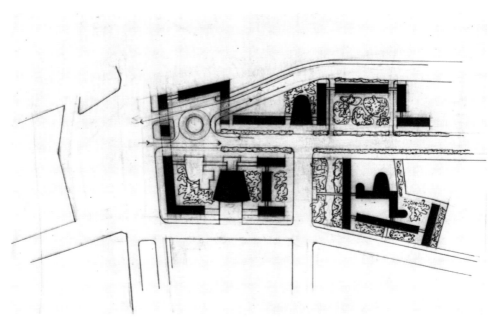

Le Corbusier, Project for an extension to the
neighboring block of the Centrosoyus, Moscow,
1928

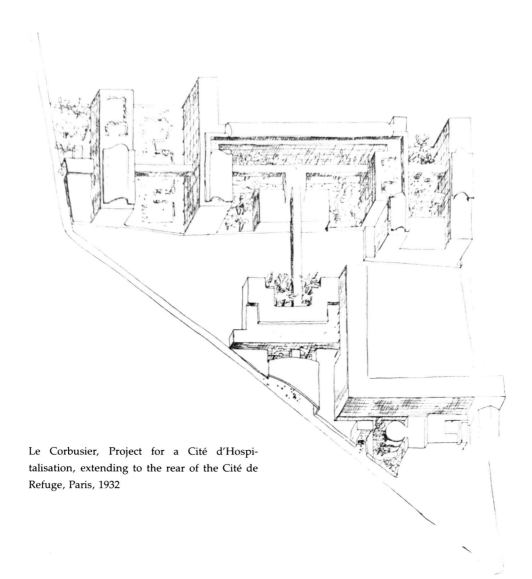

123

Le Corbusier, Project for a Cité d'Hospitalisation, extending to the rear of the Cité de
Refuge, Paris, 1932

Le Corbusier, Plan for Porte de Saint-Cloud, 1938

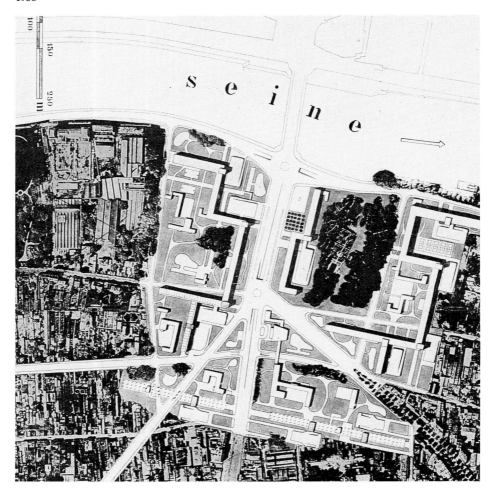

between the status of *objets-types* or "organs" of the new city and that of urban texture or ground against which other *objets-types* might stand out as figures.

The ambiguity of these extensions invites an examination of the compositional principles of Le Corbusier's *grands travaux* of the interwar years. The purpose is to discover how these principles were used to reconcile the disparate and often contradictory needs he had to satisfy in the buildings. These can be summarized as: (1) the need for the building to adapt to a specific site within a given urban context; (2) the need to create a building of symbolic presence; and (3) the need to establish the building as the representative of a type.

The main compositional principle of the four public buildings studied in this essay is *elementarization*. It distinguishes them from traditional schemes with closed courtyards, where the programmatic volumes are not distinct from each other. In Le Corbusier's *partis* for his *grands travaux*, each program element is given its own form and is clearly articulated from its neighbor. The principal elements are linear bars (containing cellular accommodation) and centroidal masses (containing places of assembly). The linear bars are coupled to each other at right angles, to form open courts. The flexible jointing permits a large number of permutations in the overall plan, and Le Corbusier's early sketches show him trying out various possibilities.

This arrangement of articulated bars is first found in the Dom-ino housing projects of 1914, where they retain some of the picturesque qualities derived from the Garden City movement and Camillo Sitte's *Der Städtebau nach seinen künstlerischen Grundsätzen*. In one particularly striking example, U- and L-shaped blocks create rectangular spaces through which a country road meanders in contrapuntal movement. This counterpoint between static buildings and free circulation was to achieve its ultimate form in the block raised on piloti, which allowed the ground level to be developed independently of the upper levels.

The articulated bars of Dom-ino were systematized as continuous bars of housing *à redents* in the Ville Contemporaine and the Plan Voisin. When Le Corbusier designed his major public buildings in the late 1920s, he adapted this compositional procedure to the needs of multipurpose buildings with their linear strings of offices or living cells.

There are strong analogies between this system of composition and the revolutionary changes in spatial organization Le Corbusier had already worked out for houses and villas. In the houses, the solid *poché* between the rooms of traditional houses is replaced by a free-flowing space interrupted only by the convex, sculptural forms of specialized volumes—bathrooms, closets, and staircases. This complex "hot" arrangement of spaces and volumes is set in contrast to the "cool" Platonic geometry within which it is contained. Le Corbusier drew

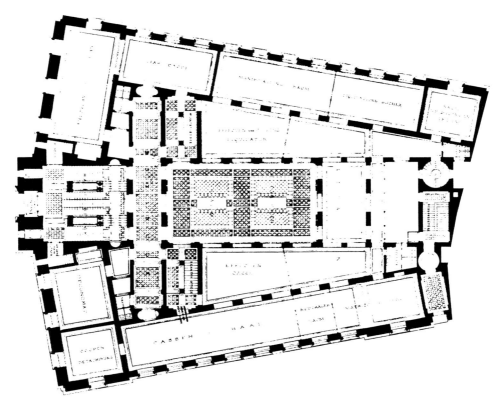

Otto Wagner, Bodenkreditanstalt (Land Credit
Association), competition design, 1884, ground
plan

Le Corbusier, Palais des Nations, competition
project, Geneva, 1927, sketches of permutations

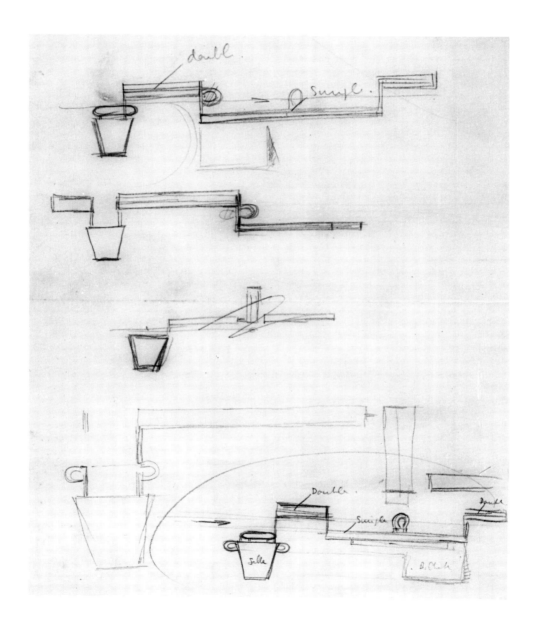

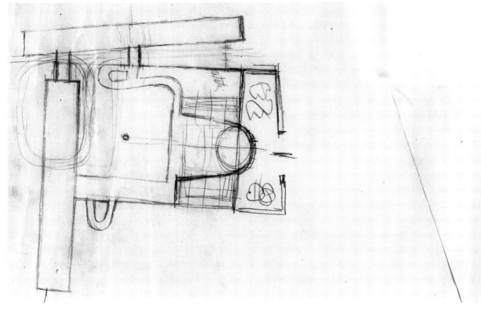

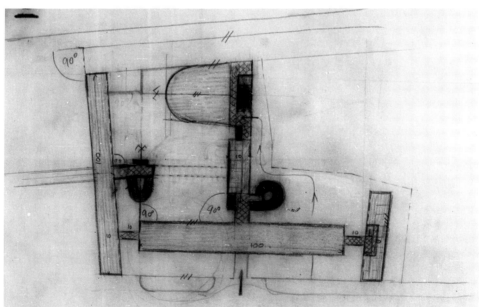

Le Corbusier, Centrosoyus, Moscow, 1928,
sketches of permutations

Le Corbusier, Lotissement Dom-ino, 1914,
sketch showing aggregations of housing units

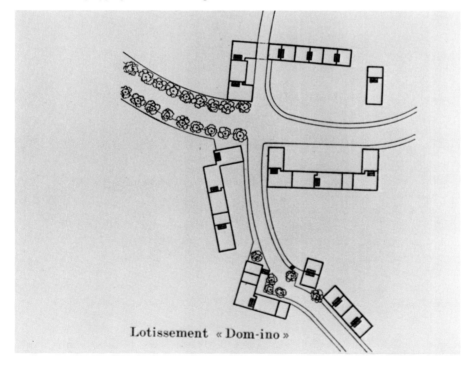

Lotissement « Dom-ino »

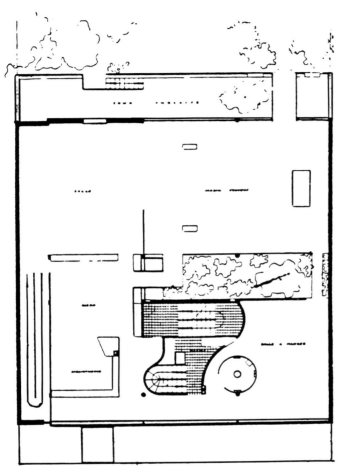

Le Corbusier, Project for Villa Meyer, 1925, interior and plan

Le Corbusier, Centrosoyus, plan

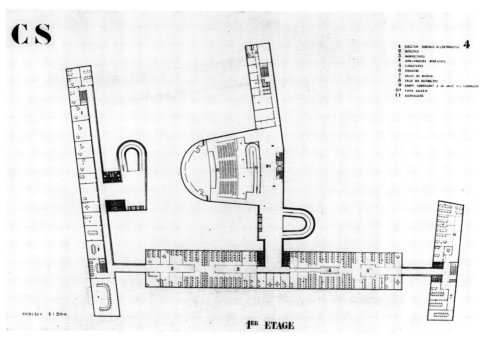

Plan of the Acropolis. Reproduced in Le Corbusier's *Vers une architecture* (1923) from Auguste
Choisy's *L'Histoire de l'architecture* (1899).

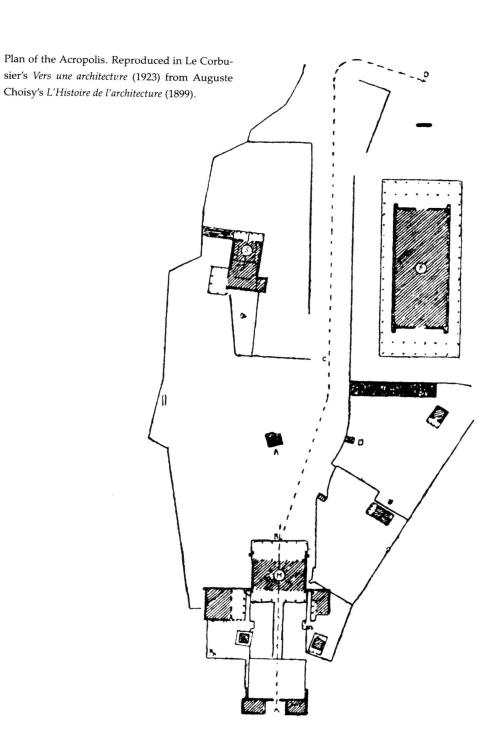

attention to the dialectic between outside and inside, pure geometry and free form, when, in describing the villa at Garches, he said, "On the exterior an architectural will is affirmed; on the inside all the functional needs are satisfied."[2]

A similar transformation occurs in the public buildings. But, whereas in the houses the ground for the play of volumes is the enveloping cube, pierced and hollowed out but never totally destroyed, in the public buildings the ground is formed by the linear bars, and the play of volumes now takes place externally. For Le Corbusier, the public building is an open-work of slender prisms defining the spatial limits of the ensemble, while at the same time implying its possible extension. All Le Corbusier's *grands travaux* of the late 1920s share these general formal characteristics.

Le Corbusier's city plans assume ideal sites, and in defending them he was careful to point out their intentionally schematic character.[3] The commissions for the public buildings of the late 1920s, on the contrary, required accommodation to local conditions. This was not, for Le Corbusier, a purely negative constraint. As the text of *Vers une architecture* makes clear, he had absorbed Auguste Choisy's theory of the picturesque, according to which the accidents of a given site play a constitutive role in the artistic organization of architectural ensembles, resulting, as in the Acropolis in Athens, in compositions of balanced asymmetry that present the viewer with a *succession des tableaux*.[4] Even among Le Corbusier's houses, where the picturesque *promenade architecturale* usually takes place *within* the constraints of the ideal cube, there are several whose external form is determined by the irregularities of their sites or by building regulations. The most celebrated of these is the Maison La Roche-Jeanneret, which Le Corbusier described as "pyramidal"—the very word used by Choisy to describe that other irregular building, the Erechtheum. These houses remain, however, at least until the 1930s, the exception rather than the rule, whereas in the *grands travaux* picturesque grouping and asymmetry are normal.

For Le Corbusier, therefore, to be site specific required more than simply making a building conform to boundary lines and irregularly shaped sites. It entailed bringing into play a system of forms and masses related to a viewer occupying specific positions in space; in short, it was "composition," which means—in the sense given it by Choisy—the artistic resolution of unforeseen exigencies, not the application of a priori rules.

The Palais des Nations
The complex of the Palais des Nations consists of two blocks—the Assembly with its ancillary accommodation and the Secretariat—linked by a long *passer-*

elle. The blocks are organized symmetrically about the orthogonal axes, and the principal axis runs through the block containing the Assembly, which presents a long frontal surface to the visitor's line of approach. This line is cut by imaginary planes that are extensions of the wings of the administrative section and that are reinforced by a system of paths running parallel to the secondary axis.

Individually, each block belongs to the species of frontalized buildings reserved by Choisy for propylaea.[5] As a pair, however, they form a "balanced asymmetry" whose outline follows the shore of the lake and whose masses offer themselves as picturesque ensembles partly screened by trees. The north side of the imagined symmetrical *parti* is missing. In the third edition of *Vers une architecture*, Le Corbusier appended a plan of the Palais showing an assumed extension to the north, its axis rotated by about ten degrees to conform to existing building and road alignments, so that even in its final form the building was not envisioned as perfectly symmetrical. The *parti* resembles certain sixteenth- and seventeenth-century projects in which long, narrow galleries are extended from older nuclei, such as the "Manica Lunga" of the Quirinale and the Grande Galerie of the Louvre—especially the latter, with its development on only one side of the central axis and its subtle shift of angle.

If we compare the arrangement of bars *à redents* in this plan with those in the Ville Contemporaine or the Plan Voisin, we see that whereas the urban blocks *à redents* are oriented in both directions, those at Geneva have two aspects, one facing the public realm of the entrance court, the other the private realm of the garden. In Le Corbusier's city plans the bars cut through a uniform and undifferentiated spatial continuum, while in the Geneva project the bars act as walls dividing the site into two phenomenally different kinds of space.

When talking of context, therefore, we refer not only to the physical context (rural or urban), but also the temporal, historical context. In the Palais des Nations Le Corbusier has both adjusted the building to the exigencies of the site and restated the perennial tradition of architecture in terms of modern life and modern technology. He seems to have wholeheartedly embraced the ceremonial, humanistic implications of the program and to have attempted to give the building an appropriate character. We shall see that in another project the same desire to imbue a building with an appropriate character led to diametrically opposite results.

The Centrosoyus

Unlike the Palais des Nations, the Centrosoyus was assigned to an urban site and presented Le Corbusier with unprecedented contextual problems. The site was bounded by roads on its three regular sides, whereas the fourth side was

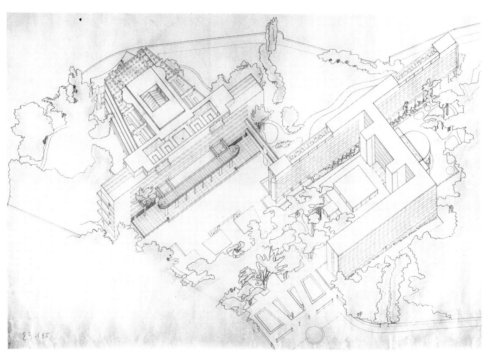

Le Corbusier, Palais des Nations, axonometric

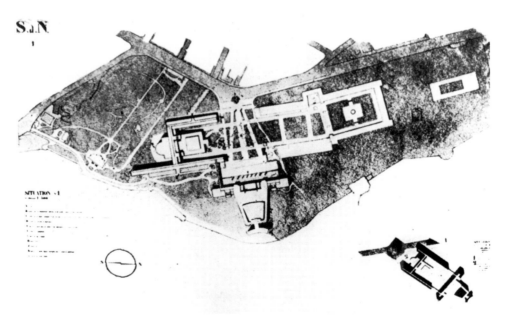

Le Corbusier, Palais des Nations, plan showing
extension

Le Corbusier, Palais des Nations, view from lake

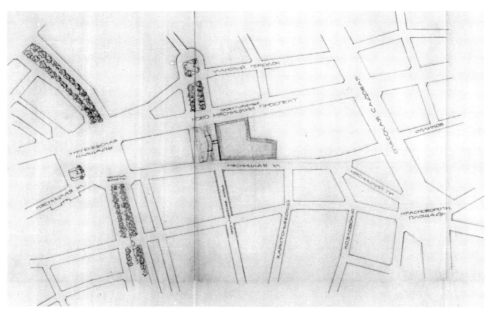

Le Corbusier, Centrosoyus, site plan

formed by an irregular boundary cutting across the block. In his earliest solutions he rejected the articulated system of bars he had used for the Palais de Nations and based his design on a simple perimeter courtyard block divided into quadrants, with the auditorium at the intersection of a cruciform system of circulation and with one quadrant omitted to avoid extending beyond the site boundary.[6] There are several extant variants of this early scheme, but in all of them the hermetic and regular quality of the plan is compensated for by irregular (and apparently somewhat arbitrary) elevational profiles and by wide penetrations at street level to gain access to the otherwise landlocked auditorium.

In these early solutions for the Centrosoyus the short southwest side is the principal façade, on axis with the auditorium and facing the boulevard with its central reservation of trees. During the evolution of the design, the main façade migrated to the longer frontage facing Miasnitskaya Street. At the same time the courtyard arrangement was transformed and the scheme began to assume its final configuration of articulated bars forming an unequal H and providing the entrance façade with a shallow forecourt.

In all these transformations we can see a persistent concern for maintaining the street alignments and for frontalized blocks, which it is necessary to penetrate in order to reach the "private" interior space. At ground- and first-floor levels this interior space is always used for vast cloakrooms and foyers, which define a pattern of movement that is in counterpoint to the configuration of the blocks above. This contrapuntal movement becomes increasingly evident once the main bars are raised up on *piloti* and their configuration becomes more pliant.

A significant result of the H-shaped plan is that the tumultuous convex form of the auditorium and the horseshoe ramps becomes exposed to the northwest frontage, strongly implying public and private sides analogous to those of the Palais des Nations but seemingly inappropriate for the actual context of regular streets and blocks. At first, even after the courtyard scheme had been abandoned, the northwest frontage was symmetrically framed by two bars—one facing the boulevard, the other holding the auditorium—and the edge of the street was defined by a low colonnade. But when, in a final move, the auditorium was rotated ninety degrees so that its convex "apse" faced the road, this contextual discipline was lost. The northwest façade became a "back" relative to the formal, frontalized southwest and southeast façades and called for the kind of rural open space with distant views that would enable the building to be understood as an object in space. Simultaneously, the overall plan became unambiguously diagonal and lost much of its earlier multivalency and complexity.

In the Centrosoyus one sees the unresolved tension, often found in the work of Le Corbusier, between the need for the building to form part of an existing

140

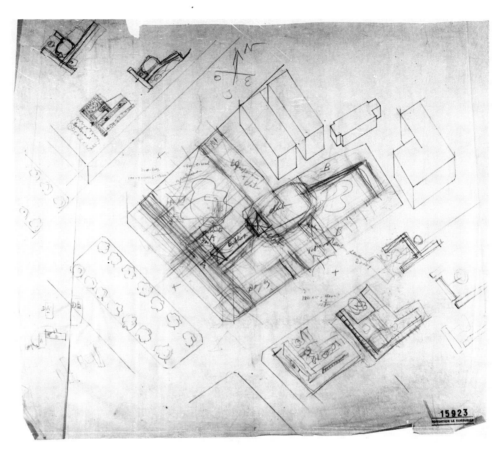

Le Corbusier, Centrosoyus, sketch for the first
project

Le Corbusier, Centrosoyus, variation on the first
project

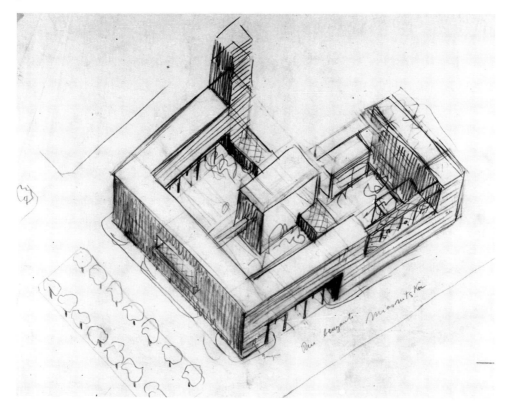

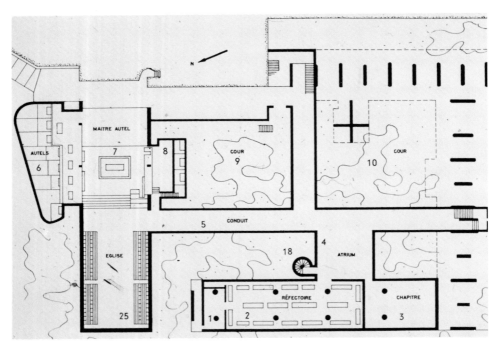

Le Corbusier, Monastery of La Tourette, Lyon,
1959, plan

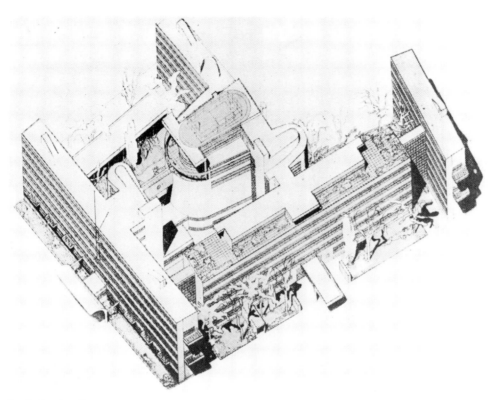

Le Corbusier, Centrosoyus, axonometric

Le Corbusier, Centrosoyus, view of the club
from Miasnitskaya Street

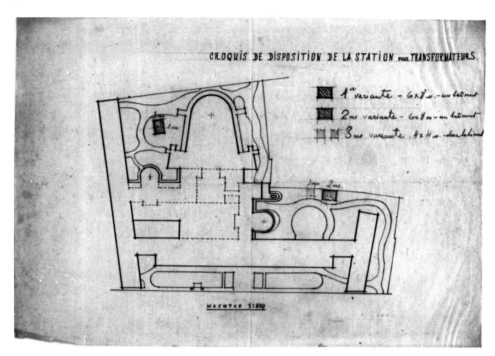

144

Le Corbusier, Centrosoyus, plan of project as
built, 1929

urban framework, to form street edges, and to consist of frontalized façades and the need for it to exist as a freestanding object.

The Cité de Refuge

The site of the Cité de Refuge cuts across the center of a triangular block formed by rue Cantagrel and rue de Chevaleret. In the *Oeuvre complète* it is described as follows:

The site was extremely unfavorable: it provided a façade of only 17 meters to the south on rue Cantagrel and another of 9 meters to the east on rue de Chevaleret: everything else was in the middle. If one had built directly on the street, according to custom, all the rooms would have overlooked courtyards and faced north.[7]

Although this passage sounds like special pleading, it is true that the site did not lend itself to a perimeter solution, even if one had been desired. What is open to question, however, is whether Le Corbusier's successive solutions did not, in fact, have recourse to a traditional typology *other* than that of the perimeter block. After all, this was a representational building and not a mere part of the urban tissue. Certainly, for Le Corbusier it had, above all, to represent modernity, but it was also called upon to symbolize a social and moral idea. In these circumstances one could reasonably expect the architect to turn to Parisian precedent in giving the building a symbolic presence and setting it off against its immediate surroundings. And, in fact, the *parti* of both the first and the final schemes have much in common with that of the Parisian *hôtel particulière*. The *corps de logis* is set back some distance from the street and consists of a block frontalized to the axis of approach and extending across the full width of the site. There is a portico *plomb sur la rue*, which acts as a sign of the building and also as a controlled point of entry to the site, which forms a relatively secluded private realm, walled off from the street.

Initially only the western half of the site was available. What appears to be one of the earliest sketches shows a cranked single-story passage leading from the entry on rue Cantagrel to a six- or seven-story dormitory block crossing the site from north to south. The east half of the site was developed by adding a second block parallel to the first and connecting them with a longitudinal block running west-east, extending to the rue Chevaleret boundary. At the change in direction of the entrance passage there was a rotunda containing the reception hall, which absorbed the axial rotation—a somewhat Beaux-Arts device. Over the rotunda a wedge-shaped lecture theater was suspended. A *passerelle*, threading through a pavilion (the dispensary), connected the rotunda to the

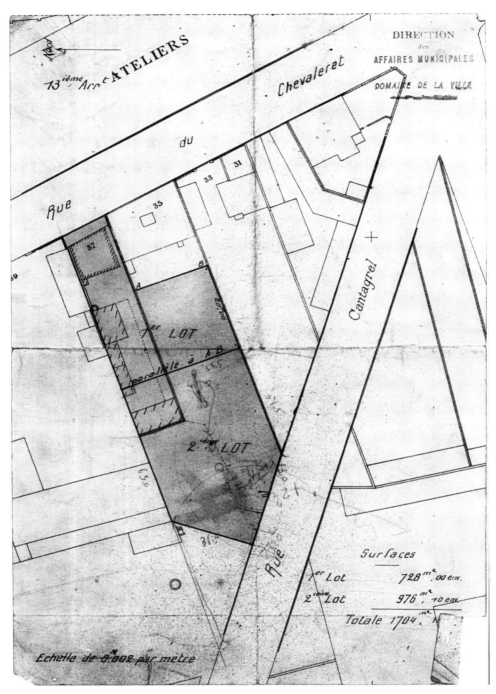

Le Corbusier, Cité de Refuge, Paris, 1929, site
plan

Hôtel le Gendre, plan. From Eugène-Emmanuel Viollet-le-Duc, *Dictionnaire raisonné de l'architecture française du XI au XVI siècle*, 6 (1868).

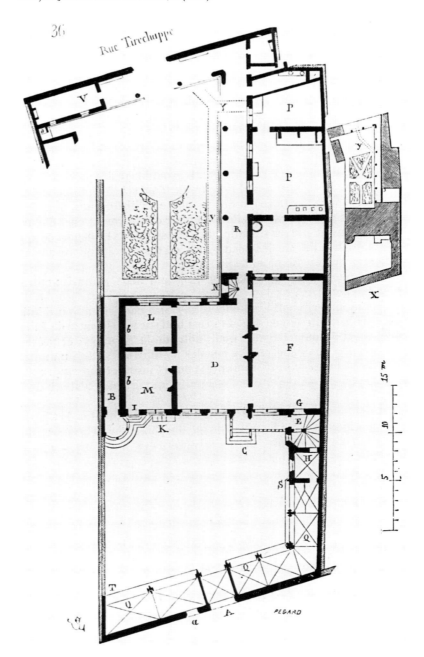

Le Corbusier, Cité de Refuge, early sketch

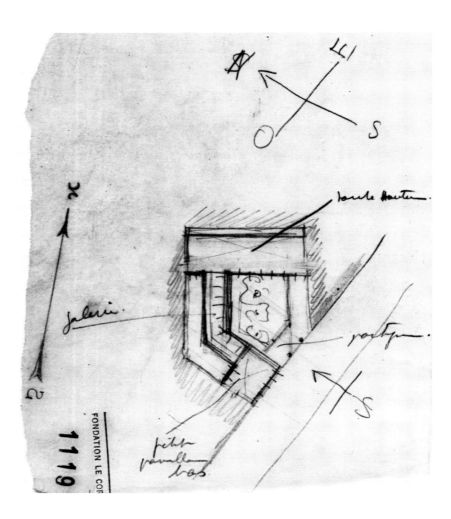

148

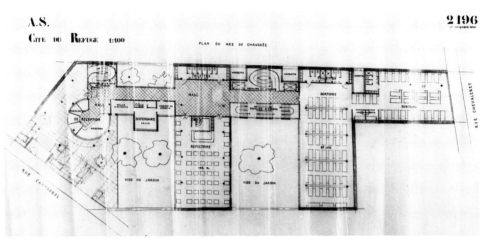

Le Corbusier, Cité de Refuge, first project, plan

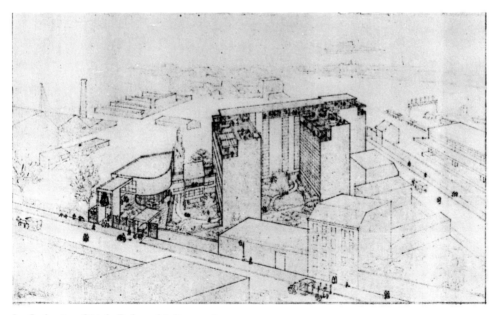

Le Corbusier, Cité de Refuge, bird's-eye view

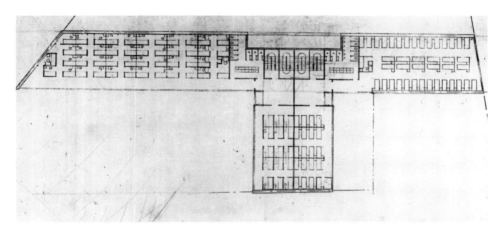

Le Corbusier, Cité de Refuge, fourth project,
plan

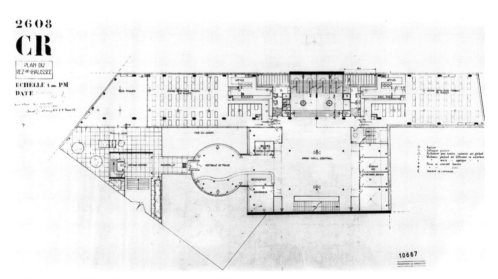

Le Corbusier, Cité de Refuge, final project, 1931,
plan

Le Corbusier, Cité de Refuge, view from rue
Cantagrel

main building. In place of the *cour d'honneur* there was a sunken garden, which continued under the dormitory blocks.

In the final scheme, the two north-south bars were replaced by a single building running east-west along the northern boundary of the site. This new arrangement had a radical effect on the entry sequence, which now had to penetrate to the middle of the site before it could be connected to the main building at the point where the main stair and the wall separating men and women occurred. Le Corbusier, however, barely altered the elements of this sequence. He simply resited them so that they formed a series of pavilions of various shapes running in front of and parallel to the main building, to which they were now connected by a protruding element containing the entrance foyer and lecture theater.

From the start, therefore, Le Corbusier had visualized an elaborate *promenade architecturale* connecting the point of entry to the site with the main accommodation. Programmatically, the promenade consists of a series of initiatory acts, necessary before entering the inner sanctum of the building, and these acts are symbolized by a series of architectural elements: portico, rotunda, *passarelle*. Yet it is important to note that this solution owes as much to the architectural demands of the site, and their formal implications, as it does to the practical and symbolic peculiarities of the program. "This group of buildings," wrote Le Corbusier, "constitutes a kind of *hors d'oeuvre*, disposed in front of the great hostel building; this last serves, in fact, as ground to the very irregular group consisting of the portico and the social service spaces."[8] The reversal of *poché* space found in his houses is repeated here; instead of a series of concave spaces carved out of the building, such as one might have found in a Beaux-Arts scheme, we are presented with their negative—a small collection of architectural volumes. And now, instead of being disposed within the cube of the building, these objects are placed in front of it, and the table on which they are displayed is tilted upward and becomes a vertical plane of reference. It seems impossible to separate the sensuous and intellectual pleasure derived from this arrangement of architectural forms from the site to which it owes its origin; as in the Palais de Nations and the Centrosoyus, the building is a response to accidental circumstances of the kind described by Choisy in his analysis of the Acropolis.

The Palais des Soviets

This project differs in its programmatic elements from the three we have discussed. The administrative content is very small, and the project consists mainly of a series of auditoria of different sizes. It also differs from them in its relation to the site. In the other projects the buildings are thought of as creating spatial

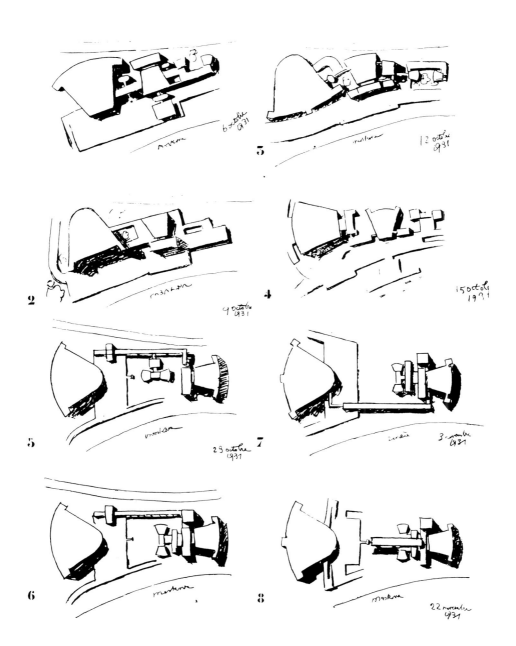

153

Le Corbusier, Palais des Soviets, competition
project, Moscow, 1931, successive variations of
the design

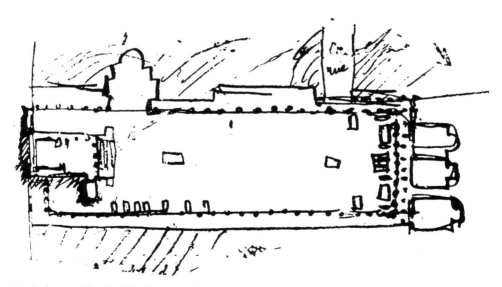

Le Corbusier, Sketch of the forum at Pompeii

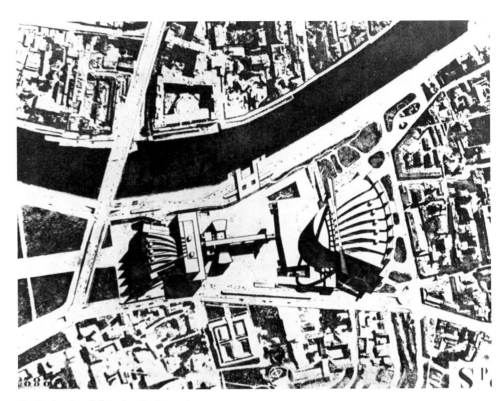

Le Corbusier, Palais des Soviets, photomontage
showing building in relation to urban context

Le Corbusier, Palais des Soviets, panoramic
view showing relation to Kremlin and Saint
Basil

boundaries. Long walls of offices or living cells form frontalized planes, the approach to which involves a more or less elaborate preparation. In all these projects there is at least the suggestion of a *cour d'honneur* and a *corps de logis,* and the centroidal masses of assembly spaces, and such, are presented as figures against the surface of the pure prism.

Despite the absence of accommodation suitable for such frontalized surfaces, the earliest solutions for the Palais des Soviets did provide an urban space—a huge "forum" overlooking the Moscow river, against which the various auditoria are lined up, rather in the manner of the temples in the forum at Pompeii, of which Le Corbusier had published a sketch in *Vers une architecture.* This solution would presumably have required the equivalent of a portico to connect the irregular group of auditoria and unify them in a single grand gesture. In the second solution, Le Corbusier still provides an urban space facing the river but has moved the two main auditoria to the sides and defines the back of the space by a low range of offices raised on columns.

In the final scheme all attempts to create a specifically urban space are abandoned. The complex is now an object arranged along a spine, like a biological organism. The spaces it offers to the city are the pure epiphenomena of its own internal structure. The complex is symmetrical along a single axis only; on the other axis it consists of objects whose configuration is explosively centrifugal and asymmetrically balanced.[9]

The spine is purely metaphorical because the range of offices, which in the second solution had formed a physical link between the two auditoria, is stopped halfway across the gap. Its end supports the acoustic reflector of the open-air assembly. The two auditoria only *appear* to be connected.

In thus interpreting the complex as a series of objects in space, Le Corbusier turned it into a constructivist icon whose silhouette complements that of the domes of Saint Basil and the Kremlin. The group of auditoria no longer need the backdrop required by the Cité de Refuge; there is nothing larger on which they can be grounded. The structural, acoustic, and circulatory demands of the complex were used to give expressive form to each element.

The desire to create a building of appropriate character led Le Corbusier to interpret the Palais des Nations in terms of what we might call "an architecture of humanism"; the same desire led him to make the Palais des Soviets into a symbol of mass culture and of the work of art in the age of the machine.

The Building versus the City

Our analysis shows that the need to adapt to the idiosyncrasies of particular sites made a positive contribution to the architectural quality of the *grands tra-*

vaux and cannot be considered as a mere obstacle to the achievement of a "new architecture." The arbitrary urban conditions with which Le Corbusier was faced played a catalytic role comparable to that of "function" in the internal arrangement of his houses.

In having to build in existing urban or rural contexts, no less than in having to give form and character to programs with strongly idealist contents, Le Corbusier was also confronted with the architectural tradition. But these buildings are not a reflection of these factors alone. They reflect as well the tension between a traditional architecture and the types of a new and contentious architecture, and they thus call into question the urban contexts on which they depend.

When experienced as part of the urban fabric, these buildings do indeed stand out as the types of a new architectural culture. That they can be read in this way is at least partly due to the extent to which they accommodate themselves to their context and in so doing expose both their similarity to, and difference from, traditional representational buildings.

When, however, Le Corbusier shows these buildings as extended, they immediately start to play a different role in the urban continuum. The use of flexible joints allows the bars to adapt to adjacent blocks; the use of *piloti* and bridges enables them to leap across existing streets, or across plots that are not yet available. The result is that the existing street pattern becomes the equivalent of the pedestrian paths that meander under the blocks *à redents* of the Ville Radieuse. A new urban pattern starts to emerge, tentacle-like, before the old one has ceased to exist. The original Centrosoyus and Cité de Refuge buildings are each absorbed into this new context. What had by itself been experienced as a whole, with articulated parts that opened up the building to its surroundings but at the same time differentiated it from its neighbors, now becomes part of a greater entity. Before, these buildings acted as the synecdochic fragments of an absent city; now they become part of the metonymic series of an actual city fragment.

However, this new urban fragment merely "stands for" the new city and can never become a part of it. Both extensions take the form of a web or matrix, and yet their representational purpose resists absorption into such a matrix. Only by denying their representational function could they assume the role of background buildings demanded of them. It is true that the articulation of their elements suggests their possible extension and allows them to become metamorphosed into small cities. From a purely formal point of view this seems to be an advantage; but from the point of view of architectural content or meaning, it is a serious disadvantage. For, while it enables Le Corbusier to make an apparently flawless demonstration of architecture in the process of becoming merged with the city, and of the consistency of a design strategy that makes such a conversion possible, it also denies those very qualities of discreteness, difference, and *lack* of continuity that would make it possible for these buildings to fulfill their larger signifying ambitions.

Perhaps this is merely reiterating what has been said many times, that the Corbusian city would be alienating and would lack the multivalency that his buildings possess in the highest degree. Yet an examination of the compositional principles of his large public buildings enables us to see this problem from a new point of view. For the real difficulty with the transformation of the representational building into a fragment of urban tissue lies in Le Corbusier's application of the same principles of composition to both, despite the differences in their scale and purpose. Because the city blocks consisted of a system of articulations similar to that found in his larger public buildings, neither could act as a satisfactory foil to the other.

In the Corbusian city it is only housing that can legitimately act as the background to representational buildings. If an attempt is made to interpret in the same way the linear bars of cellular office space in his public buildings, the buildings start to disintegrate. All that is left as a possible representation of the public realm is that part of each structure that consists of places of public assembly, etc. Only these can project, in their concentrated forms, the social meanings that the architecture of the city ought to provide. Yet, in the Corbusian scheme, it is only within the individual building that such a meaning can develop—that building whose abstract and neutral ranges of accommodation provide the necessary ground against which the dynamic figures generated by function can be displayed.

It is in this sense that the Corbusian city seems to lack any strategy by which representational buildings could continue to exist. The *grands travaux* of the late 1920s, with their original and seductive forms and their plenitude of meaning, thus seem to exist in an ambiguous and metaphorical world halfway between the existing city, of which they are a critique, and the city of the future, in which they would cease to exist.

Notes

1 See Jean-Louis Cohen, "Le Corbusier and the Mystique of the U.S.S.R.," *Oppositions* 23 (Winter 1981): 85–121.

2 Le Corbusier and Pierre Jeanneret, *Oeuvre complète 1910–1929* (Zurich: Editions Girsberger, 1935), p. 189.

3 See Le Corbusier, *Urbanisme* (Paris: Editions Crès, 1924), p. 158.

4 Cf. Auguste Choisy, *L'Histoire de l'architecture* (Paris, 1899), *Architecture Grecque;* chap. 11, "La pittoresque dans l'art Grecque." In *Vers une architecture* Le Corbusier not only printed several engravings from the *Histoire* but also paraphrased much of its picturesque theory, particularly in the chapters "Trois rappels à messieurs les architectes/III Le plan," and "Architecture/II L'illusion des plans." See also Reyner Banham, *Theory and Design in the First Machine Age* (London: The Architectural Press, 1960), chap. 2.

5 Choisy, "La pittoresque dans l'art Grecque."

6 Despite Le Corbusier's tendency toward elementarism, the courtyard building is a recurrent type in his work. It occurs for the first time in the "Immeubles Villas" of 1922 (though these were dropped in his later city plans), and it formed the basis of two buildings in the Mundaneum project: the large cloister surrounding the university and the exhibition buildings based on the theme "continents, nations, cities." In his later work the most outstanding example of this type is the monastery at Eveux, in which, as in the early schemes for the Centrosoyus, the interior of the court is opened to the outside at the lower levels and divided into quadrants.

7 Le Corbusier, *Oeuvre complète 1929–1934* (Zurich: Editions Girsberger, 1964), p. 98.

8 Ibid.

9 This uniaxiality is also a characteristic of the plan of the Ville Radieuse, which was initiated as a result of Le Corbusier's contacts with Moscow; see Cohen, "Le Corbusier and the Mystique of the U.S.S.R." The metaphor of biological structure and growth is similar in both cases.

The Significance of Le Corbusier

Le Corbusier, more than any other architect of the modern movement, insisted that architecture was the product of the individual creative intelligence. The order it created was ideal, not pragmatic. If he said, "The house is a machine for living in," it was not so much to annex architecture to a branch of empirical science as to use the machine as a model for a work of art whose form and structure were determined by laws internal to itself. The laws which applied to technology were different from those which applied to architecture, the first being directed to the solution of practical problems, the second to the creation of states of mind. In both cases, however, the desired results could be obtained only by understanding the laws which controlled their production. From this point of view Le Corbusier's famous statement can be interpreted as a metaphor for an aesthetic theory which underlay avant-garde art in general, and which had been anticipated in Konrad Fiedler's concept of the "opacity" of the work of art.[1] Le Corbusier and Ozenfant reformulated this theory in their discussion of Cubism: "In true Cubism there is something organic that passes from the interior to the exterior. Cubism was the first to want to make the picture an object, and not a species of panorama as in old painting."[2] But the analogy made by Le Corbusier between a building and a machine was more than a poetic metaphor; it was based on the assumption of an ontological identity between science and art. For the first time—so we can reconstruct the implicit argu-

Originally published in *The Le Corbusier Archive,* ed. H. Allen Brooks, vol. 1 (New York: Garland Publishing, 1984).

Nautilus Shell. From Le Corbusier, *Urbanisme* (1924).

Ventilating fan. From Le Corbusier, *Vers une architecture* (1923).

Pablo Picasso, *The Violin*, 1913. Philadelphia
Museum of Art, A. E. Gallatin Collection.

ment—technology and architecture, reality and its representation, could be seen as converging. Technology, freed from the domination of brute and intractable matter by the application of scientific laws, was approaching the condition of immateriality. Its products no longer demonstrated the conflict between matter and spirit, as in the Renaissance; they adumbrated the dissolution of matter *into* spirit. Architecture, as an art, no longer had the task of creating meaning by means of signs attached to the surfaces of the buildings. The "meaning" of architecture was now immanent in the pure forms the new technology made possible. Like a *poesis* in which words are identical to the ideas they represent, architecture had no more need of the mediating role of conventional and arbitrary signs; it would become its own sign. In this fundamental belief of "functional" architecture we see both a reflection of modernist dogma in general and a special ingredient, connecting this dogma to progress and technology and bringing to the forefront redemptive and eschatological themes that were often merely recessive in the other arts. Architecture was to be not only the symbol but also the instrument of a new society.

But if the fusion of art and technology was at the basis of modern theory, in the case of Le Corbusier it was combined with a concept of architecture derived from an older tradition—that of classicism. According to this view, architectural value could be measured only against an absolute and timeless standard. The test of technology was not only that it released new energies but that it made possible a return to the fundamental and ahistorical principles of architecture, as exemplified in the great "classical" periods—calm periods in which the means available were exactly equal to the ends desired.

The theory of architecture put forward in Le Corbusier's articles in *L'Esprit Nouveau* in the early 1920s was, in fact, an attempt to fuse two contradictory points of view—one stemming from the tradition of seventeenth-century classical thought, and the other from German idealist historicism. According to the first, architectural value rests on eternal principles and natural law, and the various technical modifications to which it is historically subject are seen as irrelevant to its essence. According to the second, architectural value is relative to its position in history, and does not depend on any principles which can be established *a priori*. In this case technology must appear as one of the essential parts of architecture, since no architectural value can be established independently of its empirical application at a particular time and place. Whereas the first qualifies the value of the exemplum with a belief in the universal power of reason, the second discards the exemplum and replaces it with immanent values that emerge from the historical reality in which they are embedded.

In Le Corbusier's *L'Esprit Nouveau* articles there is an unresolved conflict between these two points of view—a conflict in which the architect and engineer appear as protagonists playing varying roles. While the works of the engineer are needed to reflect the underlying mathematical order of the universe, the engineer is also seen as representing the blind forces of history and as working toward the solution of practical problems. His works constitute the highest collective achievement of mankind and tend toward the rational organization of society. On the other hand, it is precisely the fact that the engineer is not consciously concerned with values and is free from ideology that makes it impossible for him to replace the artist-architect, whose task is to satisfy a longing for images of the ideal. It is thus that Le Corbusier justifies the role of the artist-architect in an industrial society and establishes the work of architecture as simultaneously a work of technology and a work of art. Although the architect and the engineer employ different means and have different intentions, they are both working to the same historical ends; architecture cannot ignore technology, as it did in the nineteenth century. We therefore find in Le Corbusier a double assertion. On the one hand, he invokes historical destiny and demands a total commitment to technology and, ultimately, to the technocratic state. On the other, he clings to the idea of the architect as creative subject who transforms technology into art, material production into ideology.

Assessments of the value of Le Corbusier's architecture inevitably tend to oscillate between the two poles he himself set up, depending on whether attention is focused on his technocratic utopianism or on his buildings and projects as part of an avant-garde, yet autonomous, architectural tradition. It is possible—and legitimate—to see his architecture, as one sees twentieth-century avant-garde painting, music, and literature, as the product of a relationship between the creative subject and an objective world, an objective world consisting both of an internalized artistic tradition and of external reality. This relationship is not based on any *a priori* definition of the ideal or on any confining notion of artistic form. To reject his work because it is thus predicated on creative freedom and because its reference to the tradition is oblique and reductive would be tantamount to rejecting the entire tradition of modernism. If, on the contrary, we accept the viewpoint of modernism, the part technology plays in the works of Le Corbusier appears as a means to artistic freedom, to the opening up of new worlds of aesthetic meaning. Its relation to social utopia is then "weak" in the sense applicable to other avant-garde art forms. This explains the continued value placed on Le Corbusier's architectural aesthetic—a valuation that often exists alongside a total rejection of his view of a society dominated by technology and the quasi-fascist politics that this view entailed. Yet understandable—and even inevitable—as this double critical standard may be, it runs the risk of reducing the work of Le Corbusier to a species of "chamber music" and of concentrating on individual works whose systematic relation to each other and whose social and political content can be conveniently ignored. But we would be missing the essential quality of Le Corbusier's work if we ignored the fact that each individual project was not only an object in its own right, but a fragment of a greater whole, taking its place in an entire system. Nor was this system "artistic" in a narrow formalistic sense: it was based on a reinterpretation of the historical relationship between architecture and the social realm. However much our judgment of Le Corbusier's work tends toward this critical compartmentalization, his work must first be seen as a whole, since its overall assumptions shed light on its smallest parts.

The dichotomy between engineering and architecture set forth in *L'Esprit Nouveau* is symptomatic of a dialectical tendency that runs through all Le Corbusier's theory and practice, where a number of oppositions are either stated or implied: order/disorder; Platonic harmony/contingency; mind/organism; form/structure; symmetry/asymmetry. Though given a new urgency by the need to absorb the spirit of historicist idealism and accommodate the disruptive forces of technology, this dialectic belongs essentially to an eighteenth-century tradition. It is totally absent in the theory and practice of the Dutch and German architects of the modern movement. (It is not by chance that Le Corbusier quoted Laugier in support of his ideas about urban planning.)

The relation between this recurring dialectic and the formal principles of his architecture can be seen most clearly if we compare the principles set out in the early chapters of *Vers une architecture,* collected from the articles in *L'Esprit Nouveau,* and his houses of the 1920s. The classicism inherent in Le Corbusier's conception of architecture is immediately apparent in his definition of the three parameters of design—volume, surface, plan. It is volume that establishes the primary experience of geometrical solids seen in light. It is, however, the surface bounding the volume which, properly speaking, constitutes architecture, since the surface must contain openings referring to the practical organization of the building. There is thus a direct transition from pure geometrical form, which bypasses the traditional role of structure and its symbolic representation. The structure, in Le Corbusier's system, is a concealed skeleton which simply provides a hidden and implicit order. The surface must be "patterned," but in such a way as to preserve the unitary quality of the volume and without the order provided by a classical structural module. The pure cube and the regular grid provide a discipline within which the size, position, and degree of penetration of the voids can be determined by improvisation, following the suggestions of the plan.

In all these prescriptions there is a common dialectical theme. Freedom and improvisation, and technical determinism, are not presented as absolutes, as they are respectively in expressionist or *Sachlich* architecture. They are seen as

169

only taking on meaning within an ordered and ideal framework, and in relation to a ground—whether this ground is seen to be established by the rational grid or the Platonic volume. Le Corbusier's formal syntax is therefore grounded on principles similar to those developed by Gestalt psychology and involves the establishment of the same controlled spatial field as exists in Cubist painting. Painting and architecture each transform a putative "reality" into a virtual world whose reality is both phenomenal and tautological. In the houses at Garches and Poissy there is a constant ambiguity because the cube of the building is simultaneously established and denied, creating an aesthetic tension which the mind is always trying to resolve.

The analogy between Le Corbusier's houses and his own Purist painting is much more literal and figural than the analogy with Cubism as a whole. In both cases a "Platonic" regular frame defines a field in relation to which a number of objects are arranged—bottles, glasses, pipes in the painting; staircases, bathrooms, passages, closets in the houses. Both objects and spaces usually take the form of hollow containers whose curved convex surfaces project into, and interlock with, the neutral field. In considering this figural system, formal analysis must give way to an analysis of content and meaning. The arrangement of architectural volumes could have a direct analogy with only one kind of painting: *still life*. Not only are the objects of a still life susceptible to a high degree of abstraction without losing recognizability (an essential property of Cubism that distinguishes it from abstract painting), they also have a certain range of connotations which relates them to the contents of a house. As Meyer Shapiro has pointed out,[3] the elements of a still life belong to a class of intimate, domestic, bourgeois objects whose meaning is derived, in the first instance, from their dependence on human action and purpose. Moreover, the objects of a still life do not have a fixed spatial relationship to each other (unlike, say, the parts of a machine or the protagonists in an allegorical scene). They can be arranged at will, and therefore stand for the notion of the freedom of the artist. The freedom of arrangement of the objects given by technology which Le Corbusier insisted on is analogous to this, and relates him to a nineteenth-century tradition that relieved the artist of responsibility for public statements and made him master of a private domain of sensibility. Allowing for the necessary change of scale, the solid volumes in Le Corbusier's "Purist" houses correspond to the objects in his paintings both in their flexibility of arrangement and their functions and connotations. In the traditional *hôtel particulier*, of which the Corbusian houses are a kind of inversion, these humble and intimate spaces were concealed in the space between the principal rooms. In Le Corbusier's houses (in which there are no longer any domestic secrets), they become the main elements of plastic organization. Interacting with the spatial field, and flooded with a neutral and

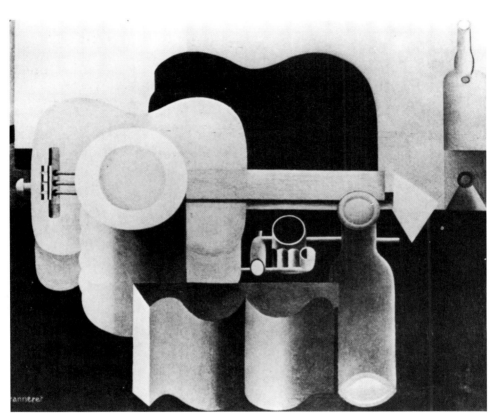

Le Corbusier, *Nature morte à la pile d'assiettes,*
1920. Basel, Kunstmuseum.

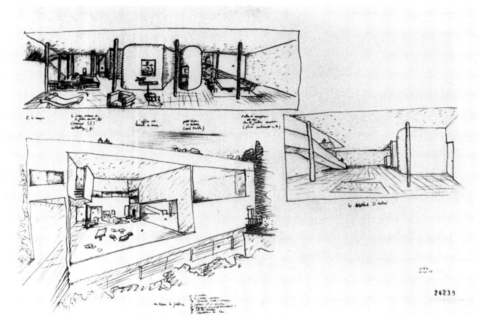

172

Le Corbusier, Project for Villa Ocampo, Buenos
Aires, 1928

uniform light, they suggest a domestic life of informal but purposeful, bracing activity and of continuous aesthetic stimulation.

In his articles in *L'Esprit Nouveau* and in his houses of the 1920s, Le Corbusier may be said to have laid the foundations of his architectural aesthetic and to have projected a new style of private life. As in the case of a number of other architects of the modern movement, the private bourgeois residence was the experimental laboratory in which many of the basic ideas of a new architecture were developed. In recent years critical attention has tended to focus on this phase of formal exploration, but, if we look on Le Corbusier's influence within a larger time scale, we see that this was not always the case. In the period immediately after World War II, when the objective conditions of reconstruction and of welfare-state capitalism seemed momentarily to confirm Le Corbusier's conception of the architectural types of a new social order, his larger public buildings were the primary object of attention. Among these it is necessary to make a distinction between individual public buildings, designed as self-contained entities and appearing to establish a comprehensive typological repertoire, and mass housing and urbanism. In the 1920s Le Corbusier's researches into the repeatable private dwelling (the "cell" from which the whole of architecture should grow) and the city went hand-in-hand, underlining the extent to which "the housing problem" was seen as coextensive with the problem of the modern city. If we exclude the office buildings forming the commercial core of the city, public buildings played no greater part in his urban plans than they did in the much less comprehensive plans of Ludwig Hilberseimer, Walter Gropius, or Ernst May. Yet in the 1920s and early 1930s Le Corbusier designed a number of public buildings to be injected into an existing urban fabric—buildings whose relation to his ideal city plans remained ambiguous. Among the most significant of these projects were the Salvation Army Hostel and the Pavillon Suisse in Paris; the League of Nations building in Geneva; the Rentenanstalt office building in Zurich; the Centrosoyus building in Moscow. At least part of the fascination these projects held for architects and schools of architecture in the 1940s and 1950s lay in the fact that they offered entirely new solutions to characteristically modern problems, while at the same time they could be assimilated to the compositional principles of the Ecole des Beaux-Arts. Their novelty lay in their exploitation of the freedom provided by modern construction and in their asymmetry and flexibility of articulation. But these new elements, which radically reinterpreted the traditional formal syntax of architecture, were subjected to a more or less traditional compositional procedure, and this seemed to give "architecture" a new lease of life and to justify Le Corbusier's claim that the perennial values of architecture were compatible with the acceptance of the most innovative techniques and forms. A striking feature of these projects was their physical detachment from their immediate environment, but this quality

173

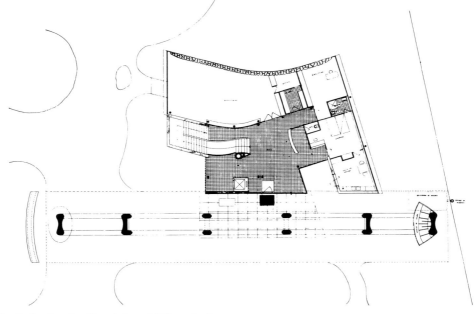

174 Le Corbusier, Pavillon Suisse, 1932, main floor
plan

was not likely to appear strange to architects who were familiar with Beaux-Arts projects of the turn of the century. Such projects were often characterized by programmatic complexity and public symbolism and were designed for imaginary sites with no context. They established a sort of *raison d'être* for the "architect-as-composer," operating on a *tabula rasa* where the nineteenth-century equation "Function: Form" could be clearly asserted. Although most of these projects by Le Corbusier, unlike the Beaux-Arts projects, were, in fact, adapted to severe site constraints (and owed much of their brilliance to this fact), they were nonetheless thought of as complete entities, as *Gestalten*, breaking the continuity of the urban tissue (Salvation Army Hostel, Centrosoyus, Rentenanstalt) or placed as objects in a weakly defined field (Pavillon Suisse).[4]

The supple and active nature of these compositions is clearly linked to the notion of the machine, with its articulated parts—a feature still found in the machines of the 1920s, automobiles, airplanes, and ships—and, as in such machines, the separate parts tend to have their own symmetrical, figural independence.

A further feature of many of these projects is the interpenetration of volumes, a kind of "simultaneity" made possible by raising the main volume on *piloti* and constituting a version of the "free plan" that allows the ground floor (reception, concierge, public rooms, etc.) to be developed on a different axis from that of the main floors, with their regular cellular subdivisions. As much as the houses of the 1920s, these projects conform systematically to the "five points"—*piloti*, roof terrace, free plan, free facade, and *fenêtre en longueur*—and exploit them in a number of ways.

Strong as may have been the influence of Le Corbusier's public buildings of the 1920s and early 1930s on architects of the immediate postwar period, however, his own postwar work shows a significant change in direction. The most striking evidence of this is the change from crystalline forms and precise detailing derived from the use of smooth rendered surfaces and steel and glass curtain walls, from which all suggestion of material substance has been abstracted, to the use of massive sculptural forms, tactile surfaces, and crude detailing associated with the use of raw concrete, brick, and wood. Although the immediate cause of this change was no doubt the shortage of steel in the postwar period in Europe, it also seems to have been the result of a change in attitude that was already manifest in his work in the 1930s. This can be inferred not only from the introduction into his paintings of the 1930s of "objects of poetic reaction"— organic *objets trouvés* and the female figure—but also from the use in his buildings of local materials—particularly in a series of houses he designed for rural settings (the Errazuriz house, designed but never built, for Chile, the de Mandrot house at Le Pradet, and the house at Mathes).

Le Corbusier, "Femme couchée, cordage et bateau à la porte ouverte," 1935. Basel, Kunstmuseum.

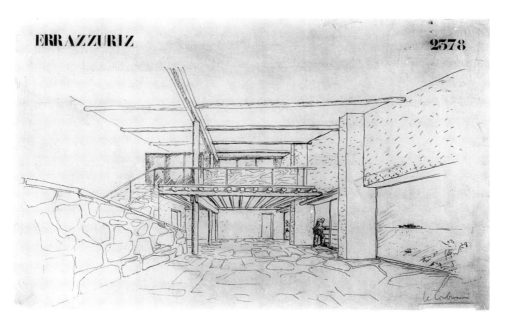

Le Corbusier, Maison de M. Errazuriz, Chile,
1930, interior view

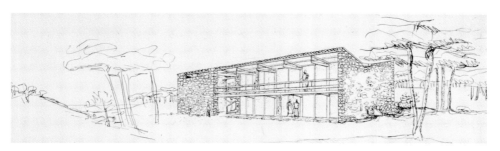

Le Corbusier, House at Mathes, 1935

Le Corbusier's loss of faith in the application of industrial techniques to architecture dates from considerably before the war and seems to have been the result of his own failure to interest either the government or industrial management in the mass production of housing. It should be mentioned here that Le Corbusier's conception of standardization and rationalization had been significantly different from that of the German architects of the modern movement, as exemplified in the housing program undertaken in Frankfurt under the direction of Ernst May. Whereas for May and his collaborators the problem was to arrive at the minimum apartment by the standardization of dwellings as a series of fixed types, for Le Corbusier the problem was to standardize only certain elements with highly specific functions, falling under the category of "equipment," and leave the architect free to arrange these elements according to artistic principles and within an envelope that need not be fixed *a priori*. This entailed a sort of architect's "patent" on the entire design and subjected the pragmatic process of rationalization to decisions on the part of the artist-architect, assimilating (as in his theory) the presumed rationality of the production process to an all-embracing artistic will. It is only in the light of Le Corbusier's notion of a dominant spiritual ideal that would give direction to the industrial process (carried out by the man of "mediocre destiny") that we can explain how it was possible for him to abandon, in the 1930s, an internationalist rationalism, imbued with Platonic meaning, for a renewed belief in the primacy of "the heart" over "the head" and a return to concepts in many ways similar to the vitalistic and regionalist ideas of his youth in La Chaux-de-Fonds. The change is clearly seen in his letter to Karel Teige of 1929, in which he refutes the deterministic ideas of the *neue Sachlichkeit* architects of the political left.[5] (A close reading of *Vers une architecture*, however, shows that this change was perhaps more one of emphasis than of substance.) The shift in view must also be seen in relation to the new political climate in Europe, in which, under the influence of the economic depression, the internationalist optimism of the postwar years gave way to nationalist sentiment and authoritarian systems of government. In the early 1930s there was a general reaction against the avant-garde, especially in Russia and Germany, where it had established a foothold in government-sponsored projects, and a return to tradition, whether classical or vernacular. Both Le Corbusier's connection with French syndicalism (which, in its belief in direct action and its concept of cultural renewal, had close analogies with Fascism) and his interest in the development of regional and peripheral cultures date from this period. Not only did he turn his attention to urban projects for Rio de Janiero and Algiers, but, in these projects, he abandoned the geometrical approach of his earlier city plans in favor of an "organic" and "geographical" urbanism in which giant linear megastructures followed the natural contours of a primordial nature and which were set in relation to the horizon of mountains and sea (a theme renewed later in his design for the Capitol of Chandigarh). In Algiers this new concept of urban form was expressive of a romantic notion according to which North African and French traditions could be integrated, to create a new Mediterranean culture—an idea reminiscent of the Pan-Germanism of the National Socialists and implying a partition of the world into regions of "natural" culture. The city is still seen as the visual analogue of a technological organization, but it now becomes an extension of nature and is experienced as a "distant" panorama, either from the vantage point of the individual dwelling or, in a more idealized form, from the air.[6]

"Reconstruction," under the aegis of the postwar welfare state, provided Le Corbusier for the first time with a symbolic and practical role that no longer depended on utopian projection or authoritarian global intervention. Nevertheless his postwar work continued to develop many of the themes of the 1930s and 1940s. In this work there is a new stress on the isolated building as a unique monument set in nature—no longer the artificially "natural" nature of the early city plans, but a nature already humanized by cultivation and containing evidence of a vernacular building tradition. There is an attempt—at Cap Martin, Ronchamp, La Tourette, and the buildings at Chandigarh and Ahmedabad in India—to draw ideas from a generalized "Mediterranean" tradition, from ancient or mythological typologies, or simply from the *genius loci*. The pure stereometric forms of a rationalized and Platonized technology give way to a greater lyricism—to sloping surfaces, catalan vaults, and free plastic modeling. The concrete frame now becomes a kind of *charpenterie* suggesting those machines reproduced in the encyclopedia of which Roland Barthes says, "The wood which constitutes them keeps them subservient to a certain notion of *play;* these machines are (to us) like big toys."[7] Whereas in the 1920s Le Corbusier's interest in proportional systems had taken the form of an *a posteriori* checking of regular surfaces, after the war it became, with the publication of the Modulor, a numerical scale that could give Platonic validity to the smallest details and the most irregular forms. The attempt was to show (against all empirical evidence) that mass production and standardization were compatible with the greatest artistic freedom, and, as such, it was merely an extension of the philosophy propounded in the 1920s. At the same time there is an increased interest in the mathematical regularity underlying organic forms, referring back to his studies of nature under the tutelage of L'Eplattenier at La Chaux-de-Fonds and to the neoplatonism and symbolism of the 1890s.

The most characteristic postwar development was the almost universal adoption of the *brise-soleil*, which became the signature of Le Corbusier's late style, as piloti had been of his early work. The *brise-soleil* was a means of counteracting

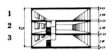

Type I

(**Appartements à 6 et à 2 personnes**) par travées de 5,50 m :

Nombre d'habitants	70
Nombre d'appartements	15
Nombre des rues intérieures	5
Hauteur totale du bâtiment, non compris pilotis et services communs	41,25 m
Cube total (sans services communs)	2720,00 m³
Surface habitable	865,00 m²
Cube des appartements	2150,00 m³
Surface d'un appartement	57,50 m²

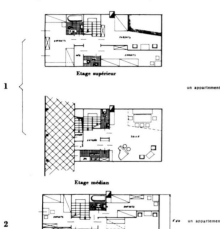

Etage supérieur

1

un appartement

Etage médian

2

un appartement

Etage inférieur

Type II

(**Appartements à 6 personnes**) par travées de 5,50 m :

Nombre d'habitants	60
Nombre d'appartements	10
Nombre des couloirs	5
Hauteur totale du bâtiment, non compris pilotis et services communs	38,60 m
Cube total (sans services communs)	2540,00 m³
Surface habitable	860,00 m²
Cube des appartements	2354,00 m³
Surface d'un appartement	86,00 m²

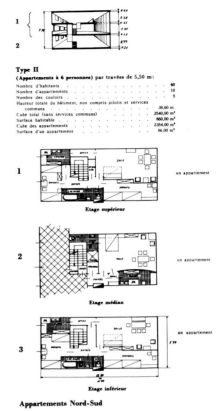

1   un appartement

Etage supérieur

2   un appartement

Etage médian

3   un appartement

Etage inférieur

Appartements Nord-Sud

180

Le Corbusier, "Ilot insalubre No. 6 apartments,"
1936, typical floor plans

Ernst May, Neue Frankfurt apartments, 1926

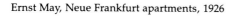

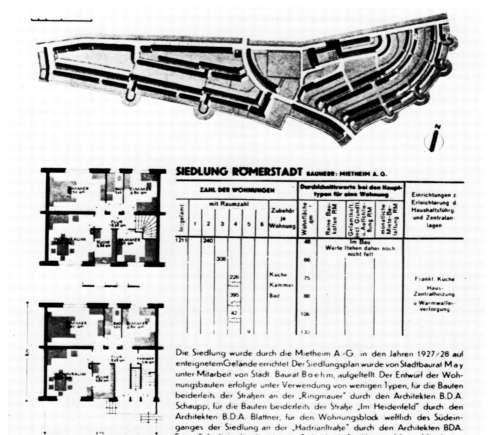

Le Corbusier, Sketch of Rio de Janeiro urbani-
zation, 1929

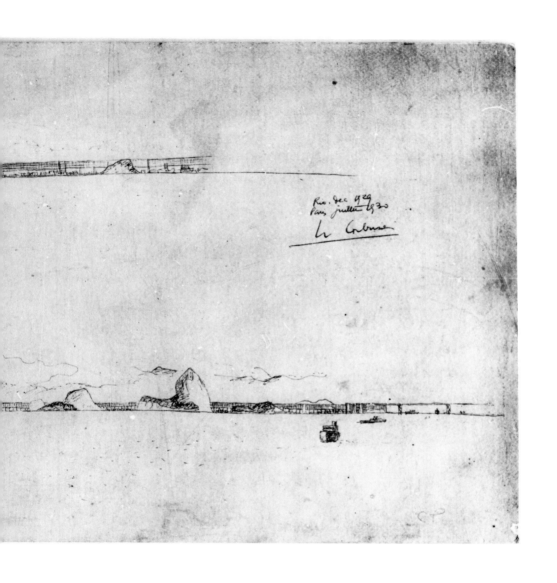

Rio. dec 1929
Paris juillet 1930
Le Corbusier

183

Le Corbusier, Roq et Rob à Cap Martin, 1949, elevation showing the integration into the landscape

Le Corbusier, Chapel at Ronchamp, 1955, model

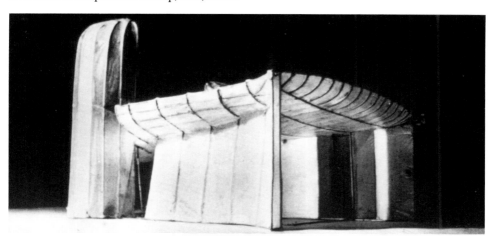

Le Corbusier, Millowner's housing, Ahmada-
bad, 1954

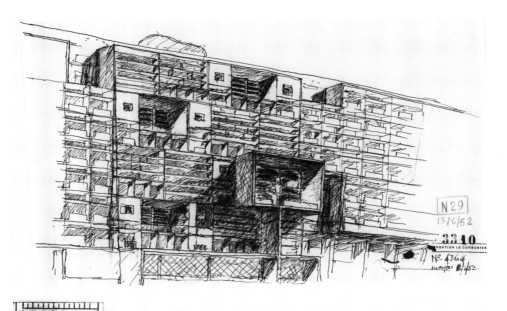

Le Corbusier, Secretariat at Chandigarh, study
of the *brise-soleil*, 1958

the vulnerability of the fully glazed facade to heat gain without having to return to the traditional hole-in-wall solid facade. In a manner wholly characteristic of Le Corbusier's dialectical logic, the ideal transparency of the external wall was not abandoned; its effects were counteracted by the addition of a new tectonic element. But the *brise-soleil* was more than a technical device; it introduced a new architectural element in the form of a thick, permeable wall, whose depth and subdivisions gave the facade the modeling and aedicular expression that had been lost with the suppression of the window and the pilaster. It must therefore be seen as a step toward the recovery of a tradition of the monumental. It made it possible to transform the slab or the tower, as at Algiers or in the Chandigarh Secretariat, into a monumental form whose surface could be manipulated to create a hierarchy of scales, proportional both to the human being and to the building as a whole.

The *brise-soleil* thus contributed to the isolation of the individual building. Even in the area of housing, the development of the *unités d'habitation* led to the monumentalization of a type that had, in Le Corbusier's earlier urban projects, been seen as part of a continuum, or as the backdrop to vegetation. At the same time, the increased interest of Le Corbusier in the linear city is indicative not only of a continuation of the regionalist philosophy exhibited in the plans for Rio de Janiero and Algiers, but also of the postulation of an "invisible" infrastructure—now little more than the mental hypostasization of the existing exchange routes of industrial capitalism—which allows for the piecemeal and ad hoc development of individual monumental buildings. The *unités d'habitation* show a continued preoccupation with the prewar theme of mass housing, but they also reflect a more pragmatic approach to the establishment and dissemination of modern architecture, in which the grip of economic rationalization has been relaxed. The objective of collective living is now to be achieved by the creation of huge oneiric and symbolic objects.

The tendency toward monumentalization in Le Corbusier's later work accentuates the conflict inherent in his work between architecture as a symbolic form and architecture as the anonymous expression of a collectivized society. The greater Le Corbusier's effort to "humanize" the unit of mass housing or the bureaucratic slab, the more problematic became the equation between architecture and technology. In contemplating his work, we are forced to detach our experience of the building as an aesthetic object from our idea of the economic and industrial nexus of which it is a part.

The sense of unreality that this engenders is reinforced by another contradiction—that between architecture considered as the subversion and transformation of the tradition, and architecture as a common, "popular" practice based on technical norms. The adoption of norms was bound to lead to the formation

Le Corbusier, Unité de Briey-en-Forêt, 1961

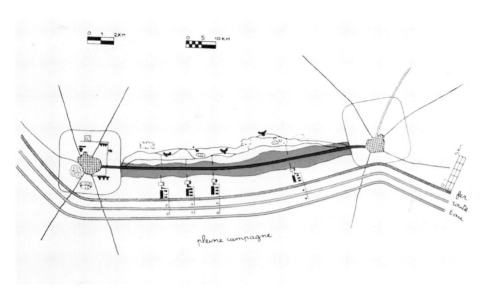

Le Corbusier, Linear Industrial City, 1942

Le Corbusier, Chandigarh, showing the Assembly building and the Secretariat, 1958–62

of habits and conventions and to deny the iconoclastic and defamiliarizing role that avant-garde architecture had assigned to itself. This process of familiarization has indeed taken place over a large area of contemporary architectural production.

The ideological content of Le Corbusier's architecture has itself been subverted by the "natural" development of capitalism and its "recuperation" of the avant-garde. We must therefore see Le Corbusier's architecture as a historical phenomenon and disengage it from its original ideological context. Its subversiveness is part of its self-contained aesthetic and remains a constantly renewable experience, after the vision of a totally renewed society, of which it was originally a part, has receded from view. Le Corbusier's architecture belongs to a "tradition of the new" which has now taken its place in our critical canon.

The split in our responses to the work of Le Corbusier no doubt owes something to the contradiction, apparent to the modern sensibility, between the abstract processes of modern life and the mythical power of art—a contradiction Le Corbusier was well aware of and tried to resolve by uniting architecture and engineering. Le Corbusier's monumental studies of Rio de Janiero, Algiers, and Chandigarh (where a newly founded "liberal" state could offer him the same opportunities that a declining empire had offered Lutyens forty years earlier) have something of the romantic and tragic grandeur of eighteenth-century neoclassical fantasies and evoke the dreamlike image of a technological world transformed into pure form. But the more purely aesthetic qualities of these unrealized or only partially successful projects of national symbolism are in most respects as great as they are in those other late works—Ronchamp, La Tourette—whose programs no longer confront the problem of power, but rather retreat into a quietistic world where art and social existence are no longer in conflict.

Our ambivalence toward Le Corbusier reflects his own ambivalence toward the modern world and is the result of the uncertainties of our age. On the one hand, his concept of technocracy and his view of architecture as the means of moral and social engineering seem seriously flawed. On the other, the plastic power and metaphorical subtlety of his buildings—their originality and certainty of touch—cannot be denied. And yet his indisputable greatness as an architect can hardly be dissociated from the grandeur of his vision and the ruthless single-mindedness with which he pursued it. If in so many ways Le Corbusier was deluded, his delusion was that of the philosopher-architect for whom architecture, precisely because of the connection it implies between the ideal and the real, was the expression of the profoundest truths. He occupied one of those rare moments in history when it seemed that the vision of the artist and man of passion converged with a collective myth.

Notes

1 See Philippe Junod, *Transparence et Opacité* (Lausanne: L'Age d'homme, 1976).

2 A. Ozenfant and C. E. Jeanneret, *La Peinture moderne* (Paris: Editions Crès, 1927).

3 Meyer Shapiro, "The Apples of Cézanne, in Shapiro, *Modern Art, 19th and 20th Centuries* (New York: George Braziller, 1978).

4 It is true that Le Corbusier shows two of these buildings (the Salvation Army Hostel and the Centrosoyus) extended as part of a continuous urban tissue, similar in form to the *à redents* housing of the Ville Radieuse. But since they are smaller in scale and more differentiated than these, they have a purely analogous relationship to them. Moreover, their status as public buildings would seem to be compromised as soon as they are seen as part of a continuum. See "The Strategies of the *Grands Travaux*," this volume, p. 121.

5 Le Corbusier, "In Defense of Architecture," trans. George Baird et al., *Oppositions* 4 (October 1974): 93–108.

6 For a comprehensive study of Le Corbusier's various projects for Algiers, see Mary McLeod, "Le Corbusier and Algiers," *Oppositions* 19/20 (1980).

7 Roland Barthes, "The Plates of the Encyclopedia," in Barthes, *New Critical Essays* (New York: Hill and Wang, 1980).

III   Pre-Texts

A Way of Looking at the Present Situation

Changes in collective sensibility often establish themselves insidiously without the support of a coherent architectural theory. (I refer, of course, to a consensus within the architectural community, broadly defined, and not to any institutionalized consensus among the public nor patronage, which, following its decline during the nineteenth century, has finally disappeared completely.) It is possible, at the moment, to recognize a certain uniformity in the projects displayed in European magazines, exhibitions, and competitions, certain morphological and thematic regularities, which clearly differentiate this work from that produced a decade ago, or, more generally, from the work produced during the time (roughly 1946–70) when the tenets of "modern architecture" were applied without being fundamentally questioned. There are exceptions that are not easily explained, such as that in England, where it is still quite usual for exhibitions to consist largely of schemes inspired by a picturesque "mecanoism." But generally there has clearly been some (perhaps short-lived) compromise between the modernist tradition and new ideas based on a reassessment of the larger architectural tradition of classicism. This compromise usually avoids the literal quotation of those stylistic tropes handed down from the eclectic tradition, which were outlawed by the modern movement. For example, it still accepts the modernist rejection of ornament, or at least has reduced ornament to such devices as alternating material and colors, which remain tectonic,

Originally published in *Casabella* 490 (April 1983).

Friedrich Weinbrenner, Koenigstrasse, Karls-
ruhe, 1808

194

Giorgio Grassi, A. Monestiroli, and R. Raffaele
Conti, Student housing at Chieti, 1978

geometrical, and nonfigurative. But at the same time, it clearly makes a connection with the architectural tradition through such generalized themes as "column," "room," "corridor," "window," "roof" and is concerned with notions of surface, limit, symmetry and difference, all of which bring into play the idea of the limits of architecture and open the possibility of architectural discourse as a critique rather than as a dogmatism. There is an awareness that, even in the avant-garde (or especially in the avant-garde), there was an element of transgression, creating a tension between a received tradition and new ideas, and that the "meaning" of avant-garde architecture lay precisely in the space between these two forces. Thus, this new sensibility seems to accept some of the reductionism of the modern movement. But in acknowledging that fundamental changes have occurred in the modern world, it assigns the origin of these changes to a period more remote from the present than was believed in the modernist movement itself: to the late eighteenth century, when, for the first time, doubts arose as to the continuity of an "organic" tradition and attempts were made to reform architecture on the principles of natural law and reason— both on the discovery of the "true" tradition and on a skepticism of tradition in general.

In attempting to give this phenomenon a theoretical framework, it would be wise to avoid redundant hypotheses—such as the one that holds that European culture took a wrong turn around 1800—hypotheses that take into account only the "regressive" aspects of eighteenth-century thought and ignore its "progressive" aspects. (These two words are used in a descriptive, not prescriptive way.) Rather, we should seek a theory that does only as much as is necessary to explain the phenomenon. It might, for example, be argued that what we are witnessing is a reversal of the positions taken in the classical avant-garde of the 1920s.

There is, at the moment, a strong current of feeling that this avant-garde was somehow "betrayed," that its utopian ideals have been distorted by its very success in the sphere of construction and real estate development. This betrayal is variously interpreted as a true betrayal (the extreme versions of this view, held by Claude Schnaidt and Anatole Kopp, among others, maintain that modernism was the true expression of an as yet unachieved socialism) or, as with Manfredo Tafuri, as the revelation of an underlying complicity between the modern movement and the capitalist system. According to Tafuri, the "materialism" of the modern movement was the final ideology of a political process that no longer had any use for philosophical idealism; the present absorption of modernism into the system is, therefore, less a betrayal than an exposure, in which what remained of the subversive in the original impulse has now been dissolved in an all-embracing system from which there is no escape.

Hannes Meyer, Peterschule, Basel, 1926

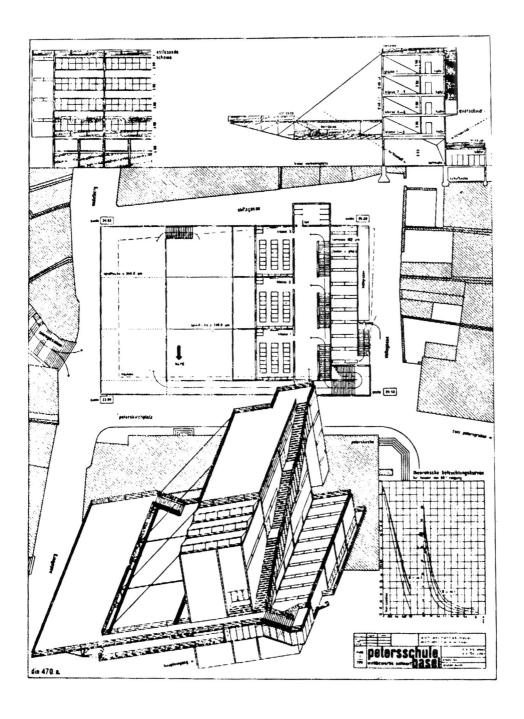

Traces of these arguments can be seen in some recent pronouncements. (It is these that have to some extent instigated the present article.) O. M. Ungers says that "functionalism" vitiated the modern movement from the start. Vittorio Gregotti replies that it was not functionalism that was wrong, but a later "economic empiricism."[1] Perhaps a better term, which embraces both points of view, would be "positivism." Positivism had its utopian progressive component from the beginning. The point about positivism, however, is not (*pace* Gregotti) whether or not it was utopian, but the manner in which this utopianism was seen as functioning. In embracing a positivistic attitude, the modern movement applied to architecture the criteria of the physical sciences (and it was part of positivism that *all* aspects of culture could and should be so defined).

From one point of view, the "experimentalism" in the modern movement had as its purpose the freeing of architecture from academic dogma. The theory of this modern movement never said that architecture was "nothing but" science and technology. What it said was that its *main impulse* should be *openness* to technological and social reality. For this to happen it was necessary to reject *a priori* rules of architecture altogether. Insofar as there were rules to be applied to architecture, these should be the rules of scientific experiment.

We therefore see in modernism a positive and a negative charge, as it were. The rules of correct architecture were now implicit, not explicit. They were a court of appeal, whose purpose was to regulate the architectural system not to provide it with a constitution. This countervalency of the criteria of correct architecture varied between an explicit dialectic, as in Le Corbusier, and a suppressed and unacknowledged system of values, as in Hannes Meyer and ABC. But it was always there.

The contemporary situation seems to be one in which these charges have been reversed. Faced with the palpable inadequacy of a practice that refuses the formulation of architectural principles, and leaves them to work themselves out within the context of external criteria, it seeks these principles as a structure against which to solve empirical problems.

It is not a question of the "autonomy" of architecture—a meaningless phrase, since any principles of architecture are empty until embodied in an action, in the reality of a situation (using this word in literal and metaphorical senses— site, program, technique).

Architecture itself, considered as a culturally defined concept, is merely a "situation" at a level deeper than immediate contingency. It is therefore neither necessary nor possible to establish it as a transcendental entity outside and beyond contingency, a Platonic idea somehow acting as the mold for that from which it borrows its forms in the first place. But this is not to deny architecture its "ideality" or to say that we no longer need to distinguish between matter and form. The ideality of architecture (or any art) lies in its ability to exemplify an *a priori* necessity that can never be given by any *particular* set of empirical conditions whatever.

This necessity was placed by positivism within the empirical. If the present situation may be said, in a certain sense, to be a reversal of this, it is because there now is a tendency to see the architectural tradition as that which gives architecture its constitution, while it is the world of empirical action that acts as the regulator.

Note

1   Vittorio Gregotti, "Common Enemies,"
Casabella (September 1982), p. 10.

Classicism and Ideology

T he return to classical models by certain architects has once more raised the question of the "meaning" of styles and their capacity to imply political attitudes. It is rather like the problem of whether handwriting reveals the character of the writer. There has, however, usually been a "normative" handwriting, taught at school, against which to measure any individual variant. A similar double criterion has always bedeviled the problem of classicism in architecture: does the classical tradition have ahistorical aesthetic value, or is it bounded by a specific history and therefore a specific set of inescapable political connotations?

The argument stems, ultimately, from the conflict between eighteenth-century ideas of universal man and natural law, and nineteenth-century historicism, which saw all cultural systems and their corresponding artifacts as relative to their position in history. But historicism did not result merely in cultural relativism; it entailed what one might call a "reversal of paradigms." Not only was classicism denied its ahistorical status, but, precisely because of its absolutist claims, it also acquired a new set of negative connotations, identifying it with class domination and authoritarian government. This negative view of classicism was one of the mainsprings of the nineteenth- and twentieth-century avant-garde, according to which architecture should not be bound to a set of stylistic rules, but should be a "free" and "spontaneous" reflection of life.

Formalism and structuralism have demonstrated that all cultural phenomena are rule-governed and that, therefore, the idea of a "natural" architecture is

Originally published in *Casabella* 489 (March 1983).

necessarily false. It seems inevitable that, sooner or later, this point of view would gravitate toward the one system of architecture that was explicitly based on rules—classicism.

At the same time, it would seem that such a return must be skeptical about classicism's own claim to be based on nature. Classicism, newly interpreted, would seem to gain its prestige more from its insistence that art is based on the mediation of convention and type than on the belief that a typology of forms has any ontological status in itself.

In fact, contemporary proponents of classicism, such as Leon Krier, tend to base their preference more on the self-evident beauty and humaneness of the classical tradition than on the cosmological beliefs of the sixteenth century.

Classicism has come to play a new role in which the passive admiration of the art of the eighteenth century, so characteristic of the twentieth century, has been converted into an active weapon against a putative "naturalism" that has no defenses against the modern consumer society. If we remember the frequent recourse of the modern movement itself to eighteenth-century models of order, proportion, and "disornamentation," we cannot avoid seeing contemporary neoclassical trends as a closely related phenomenon, although no longer tied to the historicist notion of progress and conformity with the *Zeitgeist*. In both cases a minority culture attempts to destroy the hegemony of "materialist" and philistine values. The first attempt failed because, obsessed with the analogy between Enlightenment rationalism and the rationalism of modern production, it was quickly coopted by capitalist modes of production, distribution, and consumption. The second attempt, so the argument goes, is proof against such cooption because it is removed from all considerations of material progress. Thus, what has hitherto acted in the twentieth century as a countercultural ideal expressed in terms of passive consumption (monuments, concerts of eighteenth-century music, exhibitions, "background" educational instruction) is now posited as an active mode of artistic practice.

The very possibility of this reversal rests on the profound eclecticism of modern culture, in which different cultural paradigms exist side by side at different levels of discourse. Nothing could show more clearly the "arbitrariness" of the aesthetic sign as it operates in the twentieth century.

Therefore, any attempt to link classicism with a particular political ideology or practice must itself appear as only one of a number of possible interpretations. An example of this is the connection of classical revivals to the totalitarian regimes of the first half of the twentieth century and the imputation of guilt by association. It can easily be shown that the preference of these regimes for classicism as the style for public buildings was only a special case of a more widespread cultural tendency shared alike by totalitarian and liberal regimes. Even

Bertram Goodhue, Nebraska State Capitol, Lincoln, Nebraska, 1920–32

Albert Speer, German Pavilion for the International Exposition in Paris, 1937

if we admit that its use in the liberal democracies was often associated with imperialist dreams (The City Beautiful movement, Lutyens's New Delhi), we can hardly deny that an admiration for (if not the practice of) classical art has been a feature of all those groups (even the most politically radical) that have tried to maintain "cultural standards." In this respect, advanced cultural thinking in the twentieth century is completely different from its equivalent in the mid-nineteenth century. The return to classical paradigms in architecture at the turn of the twentieth century, related to the neo-Kantian movement in philosophy and art history, was a complex event covering the whole political spectrum. It was equally capable of serving American, British, and Prussian commercial imperialism and the aspirations of social democracy in Scandinavia. It was linked equally to the rhetoric of "statehood" and to the vernacular tradition.

The facts suggest that classicism cannot be identified objectively with any particular content or ideology, but that rather it is an architectural tradition capable of attracting a host of different and contradictory meanings within the same broad cultural environment.

All returns to classicism no doubt have one notion in common: the idea that it is impossible to create an architectural language *ex nihilo*. But there is another idea that every moment of neoclassicism shares, which is that there is a single, normative tradition in European architecture. Whatever immediate tactics may be its motivation, neoclassicism has always been a return to this normative tradition—a tradition that has once and for all established the boundaries of architecture as an art.

There seem to be two ways in which this idea has made its appearance in the twentieth century. It can assume that classicism is a figural tradition whose recovery involved the notion of imitation, even if one allows this imitation a certain amount of license. This is the sense in which we must interpret such varied phenomena as the Scandinavian neoclassicism of the 1920s and 1930s, the classicism of the traditional Socialist and Fascist regimes, and that of certain contemporary architects, notably Leon Krier. The meaning of classicism here cannot be separated from the notion of its "reproduceability." Alternatively, it can accept modern constructional techniques and programs as in some sense determining, and interpret these in terms of classical principles. Here the meaning of classicism is either abstract and ahistorical, or, insofar as it refers to a figural classicism, it relies on ellipsis and irony (as with certain columns and pediments in Aldo Rossi's work, which remain detached and enigmatic, bursts of memory that refuse to be integrated as a synecdoche).

Indeed, it would seem that contemporary classicism can be measured by the extent to which the architect brings irony to the problem of relating the modern world to the values of the past.

Regionalism and Technology

Recently there have been, once again, calls for a new regionalism in architecture. These vary (to take only two examples emanating from America) from Robert Stern's belief in the possibility of an American regionalism drawing on ethnic traditions, to Kenneth Frampton's promotion of a "critical regionalism" in which what is celebrated would seem to be more the *loss* of authenticity than its recovery. But, like the regionalist philosophies which sprang up from within the ideology of modernism in the 1930s and 1950s, the new regionalist doctrines are all based on the idea of a return (whether reducible to the rhetorical modes of the comic or the ironic) to an artisanal architecture that somehow symbolizes a cultural "essence" smothered by universal technology. This urge has a surprisingly old genealogy, going back to the romantic movement at the time of the French and Industrial revolutions. It suggests some sort of historical blockage in which the terms of the same debate keep on recurring without any substantial change. All regionalists seem to speak with the voices of the Schlegel brothers and Pugin.

But there is another phenomenon which might equally be called "regionalism" that has nothing to do with any vernacular utopia or any critique of industrialism. This regionalism exists as part of the unconscious ideologies underlying current practice and is connected with the actual political economic situation whose modalities are only indirectly related to any supposedly indig-

Originally published in *Casabella* 491 (May 1983).

enous culture. It is the result of a complex interaction between modern international capitalism and various national traditions ingrained in institutions and attitudes. We should not expect to find, in this sort of regionalism, any differences of a fundamental kind, or complete survivals. Rather it manifests itself in the form of nuances. The materials of culture are similar in all cases, but each country tends to interpret these materials in a slightly different way. It is precisely because the ingredients of contemporary architecture are so similar all over the "developed" world that the slight differences of interpretation to which they are subjected in different countries are so interesting. Needless to say, the kind of regionalism I refer to has nothing to do with the old "regions of culture" attributed to ethnic characteristics, climate, language, and so on. Their areas of demarcation, on the contrary, are the most obvious and banal divisions of the modern political world, in which the nation-state is a reality. It is a regionalism based on politics. It seems curious that whenever regionalism is mentioned it is never these obvious regions of the political world that are referred to, but some imaginary entity, whose value is that it deflects attention from the most typical products of the twentieth century. If this phenomenon could be called utopian, the new and existent regionalism is more like a pathology.

One of the ways in which it manifests itself is in differences of attitude toward the relationship between technology and "architecture," where technology is taken as an external force acting on a cultural concept that has become professionally institutionalized. One of the most striking regional distinctions lies in the differences between American and European interpretations of this interaction. The American attitude toward technology has always been relaxed and pragmatic, whereas that of Europe has been idealistic. In a recent exhibition at the Museum of Modern Art in New York, this contrast was once again underlined. The exhibit consisted of four skyscraper projects, three of which were American and one English. The American examples (by Philip Johnson, Cesar Pelli, and Gordon Bunshaft) were all concerned with the problems of external configuration and surface. The buildings were conceived as consisting of a given, maximized volume, wrapped with a skin. The main problems were whether there should be more than one tower, what configuration the tower or towers should be given, and what interpretation should be given to a more or less opaque surface bounding the volumes. In recent American skyscrapers, design decisions have mostly been based on the idea of the volume as a parameter given by economics, the "architectural" problem lying in the nature of the surface enclosing this volume. No longer satisfied with the pure cube sheathed in a fully glazed curtain wall, architects have sought to give "character" to skyscrapers either through the manipulation of the shape of the tower or through the ornamental treatment of the skin. From this general perspective, recent ex-

Amancio Williams, Suspended Building for
Offices, 1948

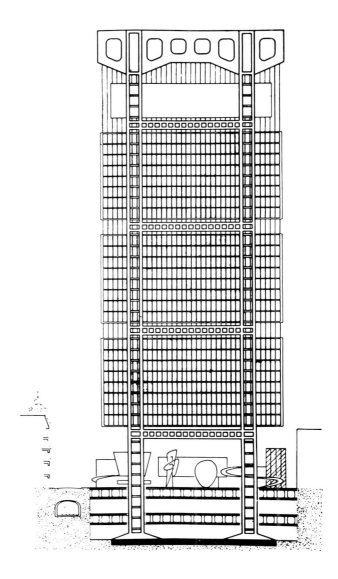

Norman Foster, Bank of Hong Kong, Hong Kong, 1986, north elevation

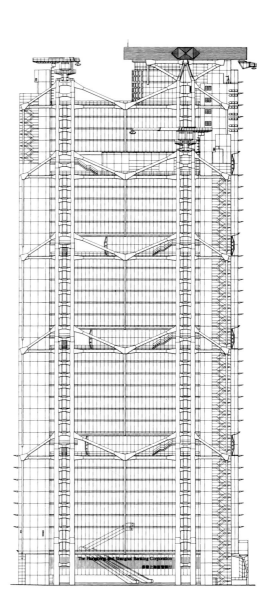

periments by Cesar Pelli and Michael Graves belong to the same syndrome. The tower is a shed to be decorated, and this is possible because the technology of skyscraper design has already forced a distinction between the body of the building and its external surface. Indeed, in recent years, there have been several cases of resurfaced office towers in New York.

The English example, The Bank of Hong Kong by Norman Foster, was based on a completely different approach. The tower was conceived of as an expressive structure, of which the contained volumes were a by-product. The purpose of the building is not primarily to satisfy the practical and economic needs of the client, but to celebrate the idea of technological progress and to suggest a technological utopia. The roots of this idea lie in prewar modernism, and the building can be traced back to the office tower project of 1948 by Amancio Williams. But its more immediate forebears are the fantasy projects of the 1900s by Archigram, in which the program of modern architecture was projected into the realm of Wellsian futurism. The surface image of Forster's building (as with the Centre Pompidou or the Lloyds bank project of Richard Rogers) is just as important as it is in the case of the typical American skyscraper. But this image is supposed to be generated "organically" from the structure and the program. In Foster's building this concern for structural and technological expression has resulted in an escalation of cost acceptable only in the case of a building whose symbolic intention was political rather than commercial. But whether or not the British government intervened in the promotion of the Hong Kong bank (just as the French government did in the case of the Centre Pompidou), the interest of this example lies in the fact that it suggests a connection between a certain kind of architecture and a certain kind of national consciousness. It is difficult not to draw the inference that the approach to technology in relation to architecture is influenced by deep-seated national obsessions. In America the basic drive is commercial success, and the need to show that this is compatible with "culture." The job of the architect is to transform a commercially viable building into a representation of cultural value, thus preserving the fundamental myths of free enterprise and capitalism. In England the situation is somewhat different. It is at least possible that the current enthusiasm there for high-tech architecture is a compensation for lack of recent success on a commercial and political level. An architecture that aims at a transcendental and utopian vision of technology can, perhaps, be seen in Freudian terms, as a displacement.

"Newness" and "Age-Value" in Aloïs Riegl

Aloïs Riegl's essay "The Modern Cult of Monuments: Its Character and Its Origin" sheds interesting light on the changing connotations of the words *modern* and *historical*.[1]

The categories Riegl uses in this essay took shape at the dawn of what has recently come to be called "modernism"—at a time when the artistic avant-garde of Vienna was calling for an art and architecture which would reflect modern life. Although his own purposes were limited to the theoretical and institutional problems associated with the preservation of artistic monuments, his remarks are clearly influenced by the historical context in which he lived and are, at the same time, sufficiently general for it to be possible to apply them to the contemporary situation in architecture.

Riegl distinguishes among three kinds of response to artistic works of the past. Such works may be interpreted as *intentional monuments*, as *unintentional monuments*, or as possessing *age-value*. He defines "age-value" as that which is "rooted purely in its value as memory . . . [which] springs from our appreciation of the time which has elapsed since [the work] was made and which has burdened it with traces of age." He continues:

These monuments are nothing more than indispensable catalysts which trigger in the beholder a sense of the life cycle, of the emergence of the particular from the general and

Originally published in *Oppositions* 25 (Fall 1982).

its gradual but inevitable dissolution back into the general. This immediate emotional effect depends on neither scholarly knowledge nor historical education.

He sets these categories in juxtaposition to two further concepts: that of the *Kunstwollen* (which attributes to works of the past its own artistic values) and something he variously calls "newness," "completeness," and "essential art-value" (which he defines as the essential quality of all new art of whatever period).

The notions of "age-value" and "newness" seem particularly apposite to the problems of contemporary architecture. Although Riegl attributes "newness" to all historical work when new, it is difficult to avoid the impression that he had in mind the ideas and work of contemporaries like Otto Wagner, and one is tempted to extend the concept to the modern movement which followed. The justification for this lies in his remark: "In our modern view, the new artifact requires flawless integrity of form and color as well as of style . . . *the truly modern work must recall . . . earlier works as little as possible*" (my italics). Therefore there should be "newness-value and the overwhelming aesthetic power it assumes whenever the circumstances are favorable."

Riegl himself establishes a sort of complementarity between this notion of "newness" and that of "age-value." He says that recognition of age-value depends on its contrast with new and modern artifacts:

From man we expect accomplished artifacts as symbols of a necessary process of human production; on the other hand, from nature acting over time, we expect their disintegration as the symbol of an equally necessary passing. . . . What must be strictly avoided is interference with the action of nature's laws, be it the suppression of nature by man or the premature destruction of human creations by nature.

Therefore, although the two ideas are antithetical and must be kept rigidly separate, they are also complementary and dependent on each other. This idea corresponds closely to the ideas of the modern movement, in which the preservation of historical monuments sometimes went hand in hand with the destruction and rebuilding of the city (see Le Corbusier's 1936 Plan Voisin for the center of Paris). Historical works have here lost their meaning as part of the fabric of time and space and are preserved as emblems of a generalized and superseded past.

It is clear that the idea of "newness" does not have the same complementary relationship to the other two categories of historical awareness specified by Riegl—those pertaining to *intentional* and *unintentional* monuments, which, as Riegl points out, both depend on their commemorative value. In the first case historical awareness is the result of a point of view "which is still normative, authoritative, hence antique-medieval, and not historical in the modern sense,

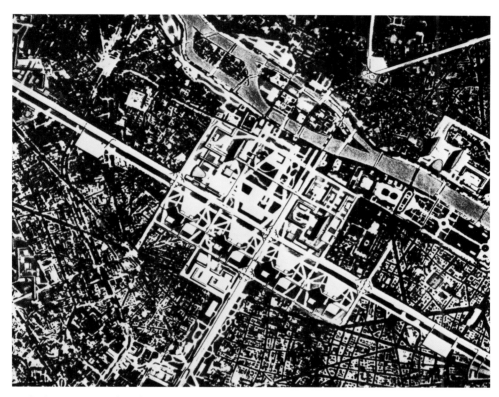

Le Corbusier, Project for a business city in Paris,
1936

Le Corbusier, Project for a business city in Paris,
1936, photomontage showing new and old sections of Paris. Le Corbusier's caption reads: "Les
nouvelles dimensions modernes et la mise en
valeur des trésors historiques apportent une
grace délicieuse."

Tourists visiting the Colosseum in Rome, c.1860. Collection of Piero Becchetti, Rome.

since it did not recognize development." There can therefore be no real distinction between the new and the old. In the second case, although there is consciousness of historical development, historical knowledge requires that the old be accurately reconstructed and be made to look as new as possible. In this historicist perspective the old takes on a surreal contemporaneity, historical time being simultaneously affirmed and annulled, as in the reconstructions of Viollet-le-Duc.

The pair "newness" and "oldness" therefore belongs to a specifically modern sensibility to which Riegl was evidently acutely sensitive and whose future he vaguely anticipated. In terms of his own thought, one characteristic demand of age-value was that monuments should be allowed to grow old gracefully and exhibit the depredations of time, though in cases where the monument still has a practical or symbolic usefulness the idea of its "natural" decay could be made to include that equally "natural" arrest of decay which comes from continued use and repair. This point of view still saw something almost organic in the process by which the new superseded the old; it did not (and could not) anticipate the onslaught on the fabric of the past that was to characterize both the ideal city plans of the 1920s and 1930s and the actual urban planning of the mid-twentieth century, and which was, as a reaction, to bring a new level of consciousness to the problem of the relation of the new to the old in architecture. Yet it is precisely in considering this reaction that Riegl's categories take on a new meaning. Although evidence of decay is no longer, as it was in Riegl's day, the most crucial element in our sense of age-value, it would seem that it is still the "age" of historical buildings that constitutes their value today, rather than their qualities either as intentional or unintentional monuments. The past is valued for its "pastness" and not because it provides models for a normative architecture or represents timeless architectural values (as it did from 1450 to roughly 1800), nor because it can be accurately reconstructed as evidence of the organic relationship between monuments and the societies that produced them (as was the case in the nineteenth century).

There are two ways in which this can be demonstrated. First, the old is still defined, negatively, in relation to the new rather than in terms of positive qualities. The difference between "postmodern" and "modernist" points of view does not reside in any radical reassessment of our relationship to historical culture; it lies solely in the fact that, whereas according to the modernist ethos the sense of the new had positive value and an "overwhelming aesthetic power," it is now often denigrated as a symbol of reductivism. The complementarity of the new and the old still persists, but one of its terms is now missing.

Second, historical monuments no longer have that commemorative power which Riegl said was an essential feature of both intentional and unintentional

The Ramparts of Carcassone before the resto-
ration by Viollet-le-Duc, 1852

The Ramparts of Carcassone after the restora-
tion by Viollet-le-Duc

Bull, Field, Volkman, Stockwell, Venetian Gardens development, Stockton, California, 1974–77

monuments. Likewise, the aesthetic rules and the rules of propriety that were an integral part of their meaning no longer have any force. Contemporary eclecticism is based neither on a belief in the absolute norms of beauty, nor on the capacity of style to evoke definite sociocultural meanings.

It seems, therefore, that we are still in the period that Riegl defined as dominated by "age-value," even though the problems connected with this concept are no longer those that confronted Riegl himself.

Note

1   Aloïs Riegl, "The Modern Cult of Monuments: Its Character and Its Origin," trans. in *Oppositions* 25 (Fall 1982).

Twentieth-Century Concepts of Urban Space

In these notes I shall discuss urban space in terms of the ideologies of the twentieth-century avant-garde compared to the revisionist notions of urban space that have emerged in recent years—an aspect of the so-called postmodern critique.

In doing this I shall use the example of Berlin. My reason for this is that, during the last eighty years or so, Berlin has been the site of particularly intense ideological conflict and creative production in the field of architecture and urban planning, due to special economic and political circumstances. Berlin's tragedy has also, in a sense, been its opportunity.

Let me first of all try to set some limits to what I mean by "urban space." Basically, I think, there are two senses in which the phrase is commonly used: in the first, characteristic of geographers and sociologists, the object of study is "social space"—that is, the spatial implications of social institutions. From this perspective, the physical characteristics of the built environment tend to be epiphenomenal. In the second sense, characteristic of architects, the object of study is the built space itself, its morphology, the way it affects our perceptions, the way it is used, and the meanings it can elicit. This view is subject to two approaches—that which sees forms as independent of functions, and that which sees functions as determining forms. In the latter view, the concept of space will tend to approach that of the geographer and sociologist, though, unlike them,

Originally published in *Architecture, Criticism, Ideology*, ed. Joan Ockman (Princeton: Princeton Architectural Press, 1985).

the architect is always finally interested in the forms, however these may be thought to be generated.

The question of the "autonomy" of architectural and urban space—that is, whether forms or functions take priority—has been the occasion of much controversy in architectural discourse since the late eighteenth century. One of the reasons for this is the split which began to open up in the eighteenth century between the idea of science and that of aesthetics, when considering artifacts in general.

Such a controversy would have been meaningless to the Greeks, who were the first in our culture to conceptualize the city as an artifact. In Greek thought the criteria for an artifact of whatever sort were that it should be well made for a good purpose. The post-Kantian concept of the work of art as a special kind of artifact that is purposeful but without purpose did not exist. It is unlikely that the Greeks thought of the city, or even buildings, as objects of aesthetic contemplation in the modern sense. The spatial organization of the city was the result of social and political practice, of action in the public realm.

The Greeks did not make the distinction we are in the habit of making between nature and reason. For Aristotle architecture and the city were extensions of the natural world and obeyed the same laws. This ancient view colored the artistic theory of the Renaissance, with its concept of natural law.

With the rise of the historicist outlook in the late eighteenth century, however, what was "rational" and therefore "natural" in classical thought became increasingly dubious. What had been seen as "rational" was now seen as mere opinion. Beauty, which had been underwritten, as it were, by absolute reason, was now seen as contingent, subjective, and relative. But at the same time, in reaction to this skeptical relativism, a new idealism emerged which attributed to beauty a transcendental status. Idealism and historical relativism were two sides of the same coin. We are still in this debate, and it has a strong bearing on the idea of urban space. Modernism tended to take a historicist and relativist view of architecture and to regard the city as an epiphenomenon of social functions, resulting in a particular kind of urban space. But postmodern developments tend to disengage urban space from its dependence on functions and to see urban space as, at least in some sense, an autonomous formal system. This view may, indeed, accept that all art is ideological, but it maintains that ideology always operates with a limited number of rhetorical and artistic devices, which are not mere symptoms of the ideologies that make use of them. It therefore insists that we must discuss urban space in terms of these rhetorical and artistic strategies, which are independent of any simple historical or functional determinism.

Before going on to discuss specific examples of contemporary urban space in terms of these concepts, I would like to touch on the word *space* itself, as used in architectural discourse. The notion of an entity which we can call "architectural space" is relatively new. It was probably first formulated by the German aesthetician and art historian August Schmarsow in the 1890s, as a critique of the theory of stylistic development put forward by Heinrich Wölfflin in his book *Renaissance and Baroque*. Schmarsow's definition of space is strictly phenomenological and psychological. Before Schmarsow everyone had been perceiving architectural space without realizing it, as Monsieur Jourdain had always been speaking prose. But although in one sense all Schmarsow did was to categorize something that had "always existed," in another sense he contributed to a change in the perception of space by architects.

From now on, space was a positive entity *within which* the traditional categories of tectonic form and surface *occurred*. Henceforth architects would think of space as something preexistent and unlimited, giving a new value to ideas of continuity, transparency, and indeterminacy. So when we use the apparently value-free word *space*, we have to be aware of its ideological implications. It is not a neutral expression. And, as I will show, it is precisely this idea of an abstract undifferentiated space that has been one of the main objects of attack by postmodern urban criticism.

With this caveat in mind, let us now look at examples of twentieth-century urban space, using a narrative on Berlin to investigate two themes: the space of social housing, and the space of the urban public realm.

Nothing illustrates more clearly the genesis of what one might call modernist urban space than the social housing in Berlin and other German cities in the 1920s. It is well known that the liberal and socialist avant-garde architects of the 1920s rejected the perimeter courtyard housing block in favor of freestanding parallel slabs. There were intermediate solutions, in Vienna, Amsterdam, and Berlin itself, in which the perimeter block was retained, but cleared of all internal building to provide spacious interior courts, such as the Karl Marx Hof in Vienna. And one should not forget the French solutions of the early twentieth century, like those of Eugène Hénard, where the courtyard was turned inside out and opened up to the street to provide light and air.

But on the whole the modernists of the 1920s rejected these solutions as "compromises," and the serried ranks of parallel slabs à la Hilberseimer and Gropius, spaced according to angles of light, became the norm—especially in the Germany of the Weimar Republic, though also in Holland in the second phase of the Amsterdam plan and in various projects of the Italian rationalists.

I believe we must see this typology as a direct answer to the *Mietkasernen* which had been hurriedly built in German cities in the last third of the nineteenth century to house the rapidly increasing urban proletariat. When one sees these *Mietkasernen* today, with their high densities and their labyrinthine and squalid courtyards, one suddenly understands the whole modern movement. Today, both in West Berlin, where they are occupied by Turkish immigrants, and in East Berlin, where they are occupied by native Germans, these *Mietkasernen* are still in use, and their slumlike condition is exaggerated by a total lack of maintenance. The continued use of these *Mietkasernen* shows how patchy the impact of the urban ideals of the modern movement has been on the structure and morphology of the old cities, except in areas where considerable wartime destruction has taken place—and this is true even under regimes in which the state controls all real estate development.

The Berlin *Siedlungen* or "housing estates" of the 1920s, built under the general supervision of Martin Wagner and Bruno Taut, were built as a critique of the *Mietkasernen*. They are halfway between garden cities and urban *quartiers*, mostly (though not always) situated on the periphery of the city, often near industrial areas, and served by public amenities.

The garden city movement had had a profound impact in Germany in the years immediately preceding World War I, when several suburban sites had been laid out in Berlin on principles derived from Unwin, the Beaux-Arts, and Camillo Sitte.

Neither these kinds of schemes nor the *Siedlungen* were thought of as extensions of the city grid, as the new nineteenth-century housing areas had been. They were seen as self-contained model "suburbs."

Unlike the garden city estates, however, the new *Siedlungen* did not exhibit symmetrical axes or spatial containment. They consisted of mechanically arranged *series* of parallel blocks, were deliberately *sachlich;* that is, they were anti-sentimental and "scientific" both in layout and iconography—smooth white surfaces, flat roofs, repetitive windows. The whole operation, from the arrangement of the slabs to the organization of the standard apartment plans, was influenced by the management theories of the Americans Taylor and Henry Ford.

Nonetheless the architects who designed them retained many of the "humanistic" ideas of the previous, more "artistically" oriented generation (many of them were indeed apostates of this very generation, including Bruno Taut himself). There are many examples of spatial manipulation to create a recognizable order and enclosure, including centrally focused spaces like Taut's horseshoe scheme in the Britz Siedlung and the long curved wall of apartments at Siemenstadt. There is also some attention given to variety of design, composition of solid and void, and a highly sensitive use of materials and color to mitigate the effect of regularity, monotony, and abstraction. Today, after fifty years of planting, few of them resemble Hilberseimer's diagrammatic and heartless projects. In fact, in many ways they seem to belong more to the ethos of the Arts and

Crafts movement than to that of Hilberseimer, or to the post-World War II housing estates of the 1960s with which we are now familiar.

A main feature of these 1920s *Siedlungen* was the concept of the building slab *in space* as opposed to the perimeter block—a figure-ground reversal of the traditional city, with its solid fabric cut through with streets. This concept was retained in Soviet housing of the 1960s. But the more human features of the prewar *Siedlungen*—their relatively small scale and uniformity of height, for instance—were abandoned for higher slabs with elevators, widely separated, occupying a no-man's-land of open space. This approach was characteristic of social housing in western Europe and some North American cities (notably New York City) after World War II. It was also a feature of the post-Stalin era in East Berlin, when whole sections of the inner city were razed and replaced with widely spaced ten-story slabs.

If we take these developments as a whole, from the 1920s to the 1960s, we have to ask the question: Does it represent a continuous humanizing and ameliorative attention toward the space of social housing, or are there other, less utopian factors at work? With this question we are at the heart of the problem of modernism, with its blowing apart of perceptible urban space, its insistence on high-rise housing, and the precedence it gave to fast automobile circulation. It seems that what started as a utopian critique of the nineteenth-century housing conditions turned into nothing more than what was needed for the success of the twentieth-century economic centralism, whether in the form of monopoly capitalism or socialist bureaucracy. It raises the whole problem of the unbridgeable gulf between what the individual can perceive and feel at home in and the vast abstract infrastructural network that is necessary for the operation of the modern consumer- and media-based society. Modernist city planning has destroyed the possibility of symbolizing the social public realm and has created a polarity between increasingly isolated *private* space and a public realm that defies any kind of spatial representation.

This leads me to the consideration of my second theme: the space of the urban public realm. There is a sense in which the avant-garde of the 1920s denied the distinction between the public and private realms, if only because it was mostly concerned with the problem of social housing on the periphery and the creation of self-contained dormitory areas. But this tendency of the twentieth-century avant-garde to ignore the public realm was balanced, in the early years of the century, by its very opposite: gigantic, Baroque-like, and purely honorific urban spaces symbolizing the state. Examples are the Washington Mall as redesigned under the 1901 McMillan plan, Lutyens's and Bakers's New Delhi, Canberra, and Albert Speer's plan for the new north-south cross axis of Berlin.

The pretentiousness and megalomania of Speer's plan, and its political asso-

Comparative plans of Paris, Berlin, Washington
D.C., New Delhi

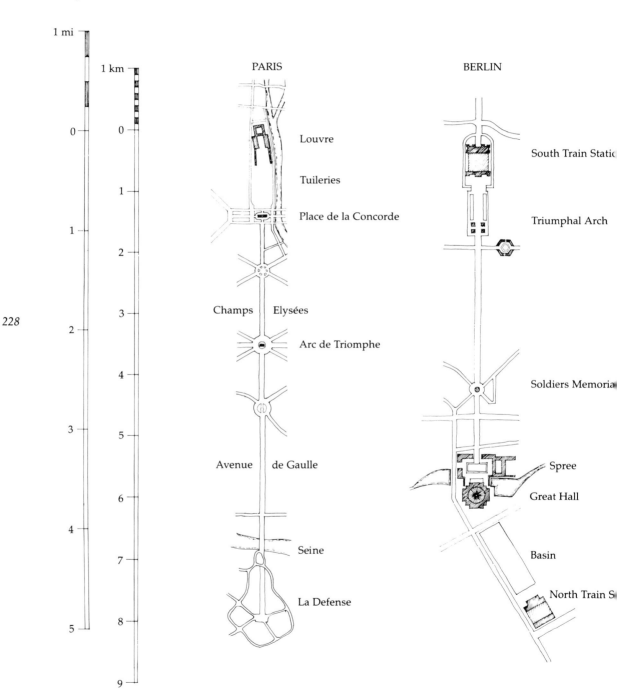

228

PARIS

Louvre

Tuileries

Place de la Concorde

Champs   Elysées

Arc de Triomphe

Avenue   de Gaulle

Seine

La Defense

BERLIN

South Train Stati

Triumphal Arch

Soldiers Memoria

Spree

Great Hall

Basin

North Train S

WASHINGTON D.C.   NEW DELHI

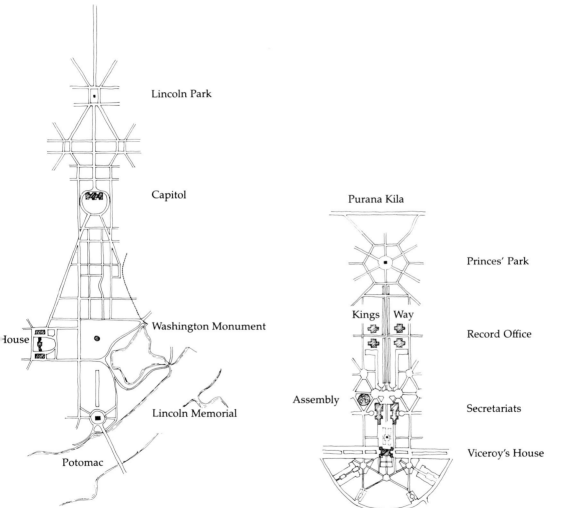

Lincoln Park

Purana Kila
                                                                    229

Capitol

Princes' Park

Kings Way

Washington Monument   Record Office

House

Assembly   Secretariats

Lincoln Memorial

Viceroy's House

Potomac

ciations, should not blind us to the fact that it belongs to a type characteristic of the early twentieth century in Democratic, Socialist, and Fascist regimes alike and that it is connected to a phenomenon of the late nineteenth and early twentieth century that David Cannadine has called "The reinvention of ritual."

The Speer plan, however, was not created in a historical vacuum. It was the culmination of a whole series of abortive projects from the early nineteenth century onward for developing a north-south axis across the Tiergarten, its head nestling in the convenient concave loop of the Spree. The Reichstag, which now stands in the most derelict part of the Tiergarten, near the wall, was a part of this historic development. Moreover, Speer's scheme was not only the culmination of this tradition, but also a way of linking the north and south railroad station. It therefore had the Hausmannesque purpose of creating an important circulation route between the two parts of western Berlin historically isolated from each other by the wedge of the Tiergarten.

To these examples must be added Karl Marx (previously Stalin) Allée in East Berlin, where, in a curious fusion of Baroque forms and socialist housing, the main route into Berlin from the east has been transformed into a boulevard.

Within the twentieth-century avant-garde, it was only Le Corbusier, who, ambiguously, tried to bridge the gap between a socially functionalized city and the city as symbol of civic or national identity and power—as is shown by his projects for Paris, Rio, Algiers, Saint-Dié, and the realized projects of Brazilia and Chandigarh.

But in the 1950s CIAM took up, for the first time within the modern movement, the question of the city core—the unprogrammed traditional city center, forming a new category not covered by the previous CIAM categories: living, working, recreation, circulation.

One of the most significant (if indirect) results of this new departure was the competition for the Hauptstadt Berlin in 1957, in which Western architects were invited to submit plans for the eighteenth-century downtown area of what is now East Berlin. Leaving aside the political role this competition played in the cold war, we can perhaps see this competition as a riposte to Stalin Allée and as a counter symbol of "democracy and modernity."

All the schemes submitted for this competition were demonstrations of the principles of modernist urban space, at this time accepted as the architectural reflection of welfare state capitalism. They consisted of *objet-type* buildings isolated from each other, or forming series, in a neutral and limitless space, arranged around the great axis of the *Unter den Linden* and connected by transportation networks. Most of the schemes were vaguely Corbusian in inspiration—Le Corbusier himself submitted a scheme—with those of Hans Scharoun and Peter and Alison Smithson making some sort of "organicist" counterproposals. Scharoun's scheme was like a giant children's play space. The Smithson's proposed a raised pedestrian grid forming an alternative circulation network, which left the original street pattern more or less intact. This was the only scheme to put a value on the existing urban structure, even though its presentation of the old and new as coexistent realities and its vast areas of redundant walkway were unrealistic and schematic. In all the schemes the surviving historic buildings were preserved but left stranded, like the Reichstag is today— isolated museum fragments dwarfed by the new buildings and transport networks.

A short time before this the city architect of East Berlin, Hermann Henselmann, in his post-Stalinist mood, had begun to erect housing slabs in the area south of Stalin Allée based on previously rejected modernist principles. The more recent housing on the Allée itself also reflects this change of direction.

But in recent years—and this underscores the curiously symbiotic relationship between East and West Berlin—there has been, on both sides of the wall, a reaction against these modernist urban ideas. In a sense there has also been a reaction in the East (or so it would appear) against the monumentalism espoused by Stalinism—a monumentalism which, as we have seen, had something in common with that of Speer and Hitler. These rejections, however, are not total. The modernist city has been rejected insofar as it was posited on urban spaces as limitless and abstract, and based on the separation of the different functional elements of the city. The monumental city has been rejected insofar as its aim was propagandist and its style megalomaniac. But, as Tafuri and Dal Co have rightly said, in connection with Stalin Allée:

It would be wrong to regard what resulted as purely ideological and propagandist; in reality Stalin Allée is the fulcrum of a project for urban reorganization affecting an entire district. In fact, it succeeds perfectly in expressing the presuppositions for the construction of the new Socialist City, which rejects divisions between architecture and urbanism and aspires to impose itself as unitary structure.[1]

In 1984 models were displayed, in East Berlin's Cultural Center, of plans for the reinstatement of the gridded street pattern and the urban blocks over a large area of inner Berlin. Instead of trying to create grandiose symbols, the intention seems to be to reinforce the traditional center of the city. This intention is confirmed by the fact that East Berlin is now in the process of renovating the eighteenth-century monuments in the historic center. (There has even been some collaboration between East and West; recently the West Berlin authorities returned to the East the sculptures designed by Schinkel for the Schlossbrucke, now Marx-Engels-Brücke, and these have now been reinstated.)

At the same time, in West Berlin, the Internationale Bauausstellung (IBA) has inaugurated a series of schemes for rebuilding in derelict areas adjacent to the wall, based on the urban block as the basic unit of urban morphology. These projects are more modest in scale than those of East Berlin and differ from them in planning logistics. In the West a number of sites have been distributed in an ad hoc fashion to well-known architects working in conjunction with local developers, whereas in the East there is a concerted master plan, with variety and individuality restricted to facade treatment. Large-scale concrete prefabrication is now being used in East Berlin to produce "classical" and "art deco" facades, in a way that suggests that, if we can talk here of "postmodernism," it is a postmodernism that has strong connections with the older tradition of socialist realism. The projects being designed in the West are less literally "historicist" in their facades, only very generalized references, in the neorationalism manner, being made to classical or vernacular traditions. One of the disadvantages of the planning procedures of IBA is that blocks by different architects and in different styles face each other across the streets, so that the street itself is not unified. But for all their problematic features, I think we can see in these developments a welcome return to a new concept of the space of the public realm. The main thrust of this new tendency is to reconstitute the city as a continuous urban fabric. It rejects the notion that every program type has its equivalent type-form. It rejects the CIAM classification of the city into differentiated generic functions, with the rigid concept of zoning and the denial of multivalency which this implied.

Instead, it seems to suggest a classification of the city in terms of a possible number of formal types or strategies.

1.   It sees the city, with its perimeter blocks and streets, as a solid, anonymous fabric which should contain a variety of functions, including housing and commerce.

2.   The few isolated buildings, whether old or modern, would gain symbolic importance by contrast with this continuous fabric.

3.   It reinstates the street and the public square as the places of unprogrammed public enjoyment and congregation.

4.   It reinforces the pedestrian scale and rejects the dominance of fast, motorized circulation.

5.   It sees the public space of the city as more analogous to so many external rooms and corridors, with definite boundaries, than to a limitless void within which buildings, circulation routes, etc., occur.

6.   Finally, it conceives of the city as historically as well as spatially continuous—capable of being read as a palimpsest. In the early-twentieth century avant-garde, the city was seen diachronically, as a linear development over time,

each period cancelling the ones before in the name of the unity of the *Zeitgeist*. The revisionist view looks at the city as a result of temporal accumulations in space—the latest intervention taking its place in the total sequence.

This, I take it, is one of the most potent models of urban space to replace the urban utopias of the 1920s and 1930s. Against this we must set not only these utopias, but also the *actual* modern city, where the image is one of chance, competititon, profit, and corporate power. In spite of its chaos—which is alternatively seen as "stimulating" and "alienating"—this city tends toward a specialization of functions, thus bringing to pass one of the aims of the 1920s avant-garde. The city proper is the place of work and commerce. Private life takes place in the rural suburbs. It sustains a schizophrenic image of the individual, who is one person in his own work situation and quite another at home. It encourages the view of modern life as dominated by simulacra.

The revisionist model, in fact, is more tolerant of the existing city than of the utopias of the classical avant-garde, precisely because the actual city is confused and congested, and still makes use of traditional patterns. Nonetheless it implies a degree of conscious ideological commitment and architectural order that runs counter to the actual city. This view has been criticized as representing a utopia (equal and opposite, perhaps, to the modernist utopia), based on a nostalgic image of past culture. This criticism would surely be justified if what were being presented was a literal model of the past, which might easily decline into kitsch or at best (to the extent that it was realizable on any substantial scale) be nothing more than a formal solution incapable of being infused with life and appropriated socially.

But to say that the past cannot simply be repeated, to acknowledge that modern life has its own exigencies equivalent to those that gave the traditional city its original meaning, is not the same as saying that the break in modern society is so complete and inexorable that no traditional values whatever can be relevant to it. To suggest this would be to return to the modernist conception of a fully determinist history, in which the past has simply to be erased. In this debate, *all* such absolutist arguments are pointless, since they are based on purely logical antinomies whose consequences are built into their premises.

Note

1 Manfredo Tafuri and Francesco Dal Co, *Modern Architecture* (New York: Abrams, 1980), p. 326.

Postmodern Critical Attitudes

The main purpose of cross-disciplinary discussions is not to blur the distinctions between the different arts, but to be able to define, and if necessary redefine, these distinctions with greater precision. It would be interesting, for example, to investigate the areas of agreement and disagreement between critics of architecture and critics of painting over a definition of postmodernism. Nonetheless there are certain factors common to present-day criticism in all the arts. The most important and at the same time most obvious of these is that we are no longer in the phase of modernism and the classical avant-garde.

In saying this I do not wish to imply that there was a monolithic critical position during this phase, even·with a single discipline. But, if we look at architecture, we see that opinions, despite their mutual differences, had more in common with each other than any of them have with advanced critical opinion today. It is true that there exists an opinion that the expression "postmodern" is meaningless and that our period is continuous with modernism. But the existence of a strong and coherent movement *against* this idea is enough to distinguish our period from that of, say, the 1950s.

But to say that we live in a postmodern critical atmosphere is perhaps not to say a great deal, because so-called postmodernism contains, if possible, even more variations than did modernism itself.

Originally published in *Art Criticism* vol. 2, no. 1 (State University of New York at Stony Brook, 1985).

I said that modernist criticism was far from monolithic. But, in fact, the critical statements of the architectural avant-garde during the 1920s and 1930s show that there was considerable agreement. The leading ideas were even reiterated with a certain monotony. The heterogeneity belongs more to the artistic practice of different architects than to differences of opinion about what they were trying to do.

One of the leading ideas in the architectural modern movement was the doctrine of functionalism. Functionalism, it is true, was emplotted differently by different schools—the Dutch, German, Russian, and French—and by different architects. But not so differently as all that. Let us take the "organic" analogy as an example. It is usual to stress the difference between those critics and architects who used the analogy of organic form and growth and those who used the analogy of the machine. Wright versus Le Corbusier; expressionism versus the *neue Sachlichkeit* and so on.

Yet both the organic and the mechanical analogies, which had been part of critical currency from the end of the eighteenth century, depended on the fact that there was a certain slippery ambiguity in the terms. They tended to become each other. The same was true in modernism. There is no doubt that for Le Corbusier, for instance, the machine itself was a metaphor for nature. And, on the opposite side, what distinguished Wright or Hugo Häring from late-nineteenth-century Art Nouveau and allied them to the more "rational" wing of the movement was precisely the notion of abstract form deriving from industrialization.

So, if one were trying to sum up the classical avant-garde, one might say that it was concerned with the functional application of abstract form. But what exactly was meant by "function"? After all, function and utility had been important critical concepts since the late eighteenth century. How was modernism any different? A possible way of defining the difference would be to say that modernism removed from the idea of function all traces of propriety or decorum—anything in fact to do with social custom. It wished to create an architecture that was entirely motivated and natural, without contamination from the arbitrary forms that survived from history.

The modernist project, then, gave a privileged position to reason, abstraction, science, and technique; and it made two assumptions about modern society. The first was that the modern period must have its own unique cultural forms with as little contamination as possible from tradition, and the second was that society was like Locke's description of the mind; a *tabula rasa*. Human institutions and forms could be rationally created on the basis of known needs.

It is this positivistic and scientistic view of society and of culture, which was an integral part of modernism (at least in architecture), that postmodern criticism has made one of its main objects of attack. But it has done this in the name of at least two widely different models. I would like to call these—adapting Françoise Choay's useful terminology—the *progressivist* and the *culturalist* models.

For the progressivists, postmodernism is a transfiguration of modernism. It carries over many ideas associated with modernism—primarily the notion of a radical break with history—but transforms them. For the culturalists, on the contrary, postmodernism implies a complete disassociation from modernism and a reaction against it in favor of tradition.

I will take Jean-François Lyotard and his book *The Postmodern Condition: A Report on Knowledge* as representative of the progressivist position.[1] In so doing I am aware that Lyotard is not writing about architecture or even art, but about knowledge and science. But his interpretation of knowledge is so broad that his essay is essentially a critique of postmodern *culture,* and it is perfectly legitimate to extrapolate from his ideas to architecture so long as one remembers that such extrapolation is conjectural.

Lyotard's critique of modernism is made from a position which is as libertarian and antiestablishment as that of modernism itself. He is still concerned with the Enlightenment project of Freedom—the title of his essay, with its "Encyclopedic" overtones, shows this—but he no longer believes that this can be achieved by the means that modernism and the Enlightenment shared: a concerted, rational "program" that would replace one set of controlling ideas with another (and therefore one set of controllers by another).

For him, the great meta-narratives that legitimized eighteenth- and nineteenth-century visions of society are no longer available. These meta-narratives were two in number: the first was the cognitive idea of spiritual and intellectual freedom, which was German in origin; the second was the practical idea of political freedom, which attained its principal expression in France. These two "master narratives" are no longer available, Lyotard claims, because technology—particularly information and communication technology—has irreversibly taken over all the positions of power. It cannot be frontally attacked, because it is, essentially, a success story, and it is judged purely on the basis of what it is good at: performance and efficiency and the maximizing of output for a given energy expenditure. Though he does not say as much, Lyotard implies that modernism unknowingly aided this process through its conflation of science and technique and its belief in technique as a liberating force.

To the extent that he diagnoses postindustrial society in this way, Lyotard appears to agree largely with Niklas Luhmann and the German school of "Systemtheorie" that in postindustrial society the *performativity of procedures* replaces the *normativity of laws.* But he disagrees with Luhmann's cynical and despairing interpretation. He believes that we can prevent the system "taking over." He does not think this can be done in the manner of modernism, by frontal assault,

237

because this would have to be based on technical control and would thus merely reinforce the very system it intended to undermine. But he believes that it can be done by action from within, because of certain in-built human factors that cannot be absorbed by the system. He makes use of a number of concepts to describe this power of resistance, this antibody within postmodern, postindustrial society. Three of these may be mentioned.

First, the idea of "narrative knowledge." Narrative knowledge distinguishes itself from scientific knowledge. It is prescriptive and not just descriptive. It is "knowing-how" rather than "knowing." Knowing how to live, how to listen, how to make. It includes value judgments about justice, happiness, and beauty. This kind of knowledge (which should perhaps be called "opinion") was the predominant kind of knowledge in the prescientific age. It is based on tradition and custom. It is still, according to Lyotard, essential, and indeed quite pervasive in everyday life.

Second, the idea of "language games." According to Lyotard there is a sort of incommensurability between different kinds of discourse, such that they cannot be reduced one to the other or to a common underlying type. Here he lumps together J. L. Austin and Ludwig Wittgenstein: the difference between denotative, performative, and prescriptive utterances (Austin), and between questions, promises, narrations (Wittgenstein).

Third, paralogy in science. Since scientific statements have to be tested according to certain agreed procedures, they differ from narrative statements, which are subject to no such constraint. However, science aims not at performative efficiency (as does technology) but at complexity, diversity, instability, and contradiction. The overall results of science are paralogical: they cannot be subsumed under a single logic or squared with each other. Science is always producing new statements.

It is evident that these concepts all tend toward the relative and the indeterminate. Knowledge is not *just* scientific knowledge. There are many language *games*, not just *language*. Science leads to multiplicity not to unicity. In a sense this view continues the breakdown of traditional certainties even further than modernism does. No global "meaning" is necessary—just multiple meanings (*petits récits*)—which are immanent in the very interstices of existence.

What about the second type of postmodern criticism, the "culturalist"? This is primarily concerned with validating specific traditional disciplines—such as architecture—rather than trying to provide an overall philosophy of art in postindustrial society. Therefore any example we may give will be more related to a specific practice than was the case with the progressivist view.

As we know, in architecture the culturalist view is marked by the claim that there are traditional values that are good independently of their place in history.

But these traditional values are no longer the Platonic abstractions by which modernism provided itself with a genealogy (rejecting the father and going back to a shadowy and remote great-grandfather). They are nothing other than the devices and forms that the history of architecture has itself created. In other words, we must build on the experience of the past in order to create a contemporary architecture.

What varies in this kind of postmodern critical discourse is the extent to which the past is seen as providing absolute models, or a set of general principles which have to be transformed if they are to be applicable to the modern world. There is nothing in postmodern criticism that can decide this point, and we find widely different interpretations of the idea of returning to the past. At one extreme we find someone like Robert Venturi, whose attitude toward tradition seems in some ways to be like that of Lyotard. Lyotard's emphasis on the indeterminate, the mixed, the pluralistic, and the fragmentary seems to echo the thesis of Venturi's *Complexity and Contradiction* and much of his architecture. At the other extreme we find an architect like Leon Krier, who treats the tradition of classicism as an absolute model even if he takes as much from neoclassicism as from Roman architecture.

In between these two extremes one finds a whole range of solution types in which classical forms are used fairly literally but are connected together in peculiar ways. Many architects are now using these traditional forms with a sense of parody (though why they should be parodied is not quite clear) or with a cartoonlike irreverence and an apparently unintentional vulgarity (but what is vulgarity?).

But different as they may be they have one thing in common—they all reject the modernist prohibition against imitation. They all, to some extent, loosen the connection that historicist thought makes between artistic forms and the Zeitgeist. They all treat architecture as a discipline with its own internal tradition, which is at least partially independent of the change in technical, economic, and social conditions. In other words, they *de-historicize* architecture.

Perhaps, in fact, the greatest difference between this type of postmodernism and the first type is that the first type is fundamentally historicist. Instead of underemphasizing the relevance of historical change, as culturalist postmodernism does, progressivist postmodernism emphasizes it—emphasizes the difference between our age and all those that preceded it. The historiographic model here seems to be that of Michel Foucault, with his notion of different periods and their different "epistemes," or of Thomas Kuhn, with his notion of changing "paradigms."

But here I would draw your attention to a curious reversal that seems to take place in the respective positions of progressivist and culturalist postmoderns in their relation to history. Lyotard would like to say that we are committed to a peculiar stage of cultural evolution which is different from anything that has gone before and which is intimately connected to the economic and technical developments of postindustrial society. He stresses this in his rejection of what he calls legitimation by the kind of meta-narrative characteristic of all traditional societies. But, as I have said, he also stresses the continued importance of narrative knowledge and the role of the *petit récit*. Is he not invoking an archaic and nostalgic image here? He says that, paradoxically, narrative knowledge, with its dependence on customary and traditional kinds of wisdom, has the effect of obliterating the past. It does so because, in the process of being reenacted, the past *becomes* the present.

Translating this into architecture, one might imagine it to apply to the middle ages, where a craft tradition internalized and transformed what had (remotely) been received from antiquity. One might, perhaps, be able to apply it to the Renaissance, when a defunct tradition was revived and codified, but soon became second nature. It would, I think, be difficult to apply it to the end of the eighteenth century, when the past suddenly begins to seem very remote and is looked back to nostalgically. It would be more difficult to apply it to nineteenth-century eclecticism and revivalism, and it would be more difficult still to apply it to the present, when almost any more or less literal reference to the architectural tradition looks like a quotation.

As for the cultural postmodernists, we see a reciprocal reversal. Here the claim is that architecture is to an important extent free of historical determination. In returning to the past we are turning to eternal aesthetic values. Yet it is precisely the use of past forms that draws our attention to our remoteness from the time in which these forms were originally developed. We are reminded of the past *as the past*. The only way in which a building could make us feel that the values of architecture were eternal and not subject to historical change would be if its forms seemed "natural" to our way of life, in other words, "modern." But in this case we would have to be able to forget that these forms were specifically historical, as was no doubt possible in the middle ages and in the Renaissance. Historical time would have, once more, to become mythical time.

Finally, it might be interesting to compare the attitudes toward the "new" in Lyotard and in culturalist postmodernism.

The "new" has been an ingredient of the avant-garde since the introduction of this term into critical discourse in the mid-nineteenth century. In truth, the argument goes back to the quarrel between the ancients and the moderns in the French academy in the seventeenth century. Then, of course, it arose in the field of science, but was applied by the Perrault brothers to architecture. "We can do better than the ancients." But in the nineteenth-century avant-garde the "new" took on prophetic connotations: art was thought of as anticipating cultural freedom, chiefly through its ability to perceive and project reality.

In Lyotard the "new" is connected with science. In calling on the "players" in the "game" of scientific discourse to be ready to accept different "rules," he says, "The only legitimation that can make this kind of request admissible is that it will generate ideas, in other words, new statements." This belief in the new is even more extreme than it was in modernism, where statements were expected to be "true" and correspond to "reality" as well as be new. (What else is functionalism but a kind of realism?)

It is probably not altogether fair to guess from Lyotard's view of science what might be his view of art. If narrative knowledge is the knowledge of custom, newness cannot be its most important property. (Absolute consistency is, after all, the last thing Lyotard is claiming.) Nonetheless there is a spirit in Lyotard which favors open-endedness and risk, which has much in common with the classical avant-garde, and which is opposed to the conservative spirit of culturalist postmodernism.

Few culturalist postmodernists would deny that modern works are bound to be different from past works, if only because the artist or architect cannot be conscious of all the factors that are impinging on him. But they would nonetheless be likely to place the emphasis on what was *not* new in a design—on the element of tradition that was being transformed. It would seem, then, that in their attitudes both to the way historical memory operates in the present and to the concept of invention, progressivist and culturalist postmodernists have diametrically opposite views, however much they may agree about other matters.

It has been my purpose in this essay to try to elucidate a few of these differences, and, in so doing, to show that postmodernist criticism is very far from being monolithic. In my opinion not enough attention has been given to the fact that the same term is often used to refer to opposite ideas.

241

Note

1 Jean-François Lyotard, *The Postmodern Condition: A Report on Knowledge* (Minneapolis: University of Minnesota Press, 1984).

Postmodernism and Structuralism:
A Retrospective Glance

The term *postmodern* seems, by turns, empty or tendentious. Probably the nearest we could get to an acceptable definition would be something along the lines of Andreas Huyssen's proposition: the movements in art and architecture that have taken the place of an exhausted high modernism.[1] This definition implies that the unifying concepts of modernism have been replaced by a plurality of tendencies and that it would be foolish to expect a single guiding idea in postmodern practice. On the other hand, certain dominant tendencies can be discerned in each of the semi-autonomous institutions of contemporary culture, and this essay will investigate these within the field of architecture. This is not to say that in architecture we are confronted with a unique set of practices that have nothing in common with those of other disciplines. But before we can recognize the overlaps and transgressions that take place across the boundaries separating different fields, it is first necessary to establish provisional boundaries.

I will begin, therefore, by pointing to two characteristics of architecture that, it seems to me, differentiate it from the other arts and that help to explain the specific forms of postmodern practice that we find in architecture. The first way in which architecture differs from the other arts is that it is very expensive. With architecture so bound to the sources of finance and power, it is much more difficult for the architect than for other artists to operate within an *apparently*

Originally published in *Assemblage* 5 (February 1988).

autonomous subculture or to retain that independence from bourgeois taste that has been the ambition of art since the early nineteenth century. To play an effective critical role, architecture has to ally itself with major economic tendencies claimed as progressive—as happened in the 1920s when "modernization" and technical advance were associated with social renewal and a utopian vision. The second way in which architecture differs from the other arts is that its mode of reception is one of distraction rather than contemplation. As Walter Benjamin pointed out in his essay "The Work of Art in the Age of Mechanical Reproduction," this distracted mode of reception—which led him to see architecture as a paradigm for those characteristically "modern" arts, photography and cinema— is shaped by the establishment of habits.[2] Thus the power that initially seems to be invested in the architect is withdrawn from him, first, because he is a mere agent and, second, through a sort of indifference to architecture that results from its very ubiquity and usefulness. These factors have played a large part in the failure of the modern movement in architecture to live up to its own program, based as it was on a somewhat fictitious view of the architect's prophetic and influential role in society.

The critique of modernism that developed in the late sixties was overwhelmingly concerned with this failure. Modern architecture had promised no less than the complete renewal of the urban and rural environment. In this it differed from the avant-garde movements in the other arts, which could only promise a spiritual renewal. Of course certain artistic movements—notably dada and surrealism—were closely connected with the political left; but only architecture offered a revolution in the actual social realm irrespective of whether or not its protagonists were on the political left (which, as it happens, many of them were). Only in the architectural avant-garde were the ideal world of art and the real world of empirical fact conflated without the presumptive need for political revolution. Architecture founded its promise largely on the belief that technology could solve the practical and artistic problems of modern social existence.

Since the modern movement intended a global revolution, not merely of architectural taste, but of the urban environment, it is with the attack on the modernist city that we should begin our description of at least one strand of what is known as "postmodernism." Many factors contribute to the reaction against the modernist city. One is the view that it was essentially unbuildable except under those inherently rare political conditions that made possible a Brasilia or a Chandigarh—and that there the results were highly questionable from both a sociological and an aesthetic point of view. Another is that in existing cities, the piecemeal application of such modernist principles as zoning, highway construction, and the welcoming of skyscraper technology destroyed or rendered alien the central urban areas. A third is that the creation of large high-rise housing projects in the center or on the periphery of the great cities obliterated all trace of the existing fabric and the community structure associated with it without providing a genuine alternative.

Thus we can observe two main phenomena: first, the fragmentary and piecemeal application of versions of the technological utopia of the 1920s as part either of welfare state politics or of capitalist growth; second, the appropriation of modernist techniques and imagery, originally utopian in intention, by business corporations and private interest pressure groups. In the first case the critique was sociological and psychological. In the second it was ideological: the very intention and meaning of the modern movement was seen as having been "betrayed" and inverted, so that advanced building technology and its associated aesthetic, no longer the symbols of a new social order based on cooperation, became a means of enhancing the prestige of big business.

When we turn our attention from the city to the individual building we find that one of the strongest critiques was directed against the architectural version of minimalism, closely tied to the doctrine of functionalism. As modern architecture was generally adopted after the war, adapting itself to the real tasks of building on a large scale, and being disseminated throughout the profession, its formal rules came to be applied in an increasingly perfunctory way. What could be called the proto-postmodern critique of modern architecture in the 1960s was largely based on the monotonous and boring quality of most modern buildings. Not only did these seem artistically incompetent, but they often failed as well to work at a technical and practical level. Even allowing for the naive populism and philistinism of much of this criticism, we have to admit that it contained much truth. A good deal of professional arrogance was involved, and, for a short period, we had the curious spectacle of an entire professional body thinking of itself as an avant-garde. I believe that it is therefore important to understand that the antimodernist reaction was, in fact, a reaction against a modern movement that had become conservative, professionalized, and routinized. It was not *primarily* directed against the seminal works of the 1920s or 1930s.

Also present, however, was a developing critique of modernist theory, especially the explicit doctrine of functionalism and the implicit doctrine of historicism. It has been correctly said that this critique was more often directed against the self-perpetuated mythology of modernism than against modern architecture itself—which was far from allowing itself to be restricted by the narrow concept of functionalism or the total rejection of history that was proclaimed by theory. But it is not so easy to separate the practice of modernism from its theory, and even if the criticism left certain modern works intact, it was high time to question a body of assumptions that had, by the mid-1960s, clearly become restricting and irrelevant.

Funtionalism and minimalism were closely bound together in architecture. This combination of ideas was not restricted to architecture—we can find a comparable system of ideas in the philosophy of Bertrand Russell and the anthropology of Bronislaw Malinowski, as well as, most apparently, in the music of Arnold Schönberg—but in architecture functionalism had an obvious commonsense application that it lacked elsewhere. Architecture, like music and the other arts, has traditionally depended on the arrangement or composition of a number of preformed rhetorical figures—what Charles Rosen, speaking of music but using an architectural metaphor, calls the use of "large blocks of prefabricated material." The new architecture of the 1920s sought to banish these tropes and formulae and to replace them with atomic elements that were considered formally and functionally irreducible. The meaning was to be derived from the formal and functional context of the work itself, supposedly independent of the stylistic clichés and rhetorical gestures handed down by the tradition.

One of the chief objects of the postmodern attack was this notion of a set of functions, tied to the particular work, but having a prior and external existence to it. The attack was not against the idea of a building having a purpose, but against the idea that the aesthetic form of the building should be utterly transparent to this purpose, defined by a set of more or less quantifiable functions. Such ideas had been questioned before, both by the enemies of modernism and by architects within the movement. But by the 1960s, just at the time that some architects had reduced the idea of functionalism to a would-be behavioristic system, a weapon of attack against functionalism became available—a weapon that itself seemed to possess all the credentials of a positive science. This was "structuralism," as inaugurated by Ferdinand de Saussure and as developed variously by Roman Jakobson, Claude Lévi-Strauss, and Roland Barthes. According to this approach the ability of signs to convey meaning, within any sign system whatever, depends on an arbitrary and conventional structure of relationships within a particular system and not on the relation of signs to preexistent or fixed referents in outside reality. The application of this linguistic model to architecture enabled "function" to be seen as the false reification and naturalization of a set of culturally determined values that might or might not be considered as part of the system of meaning constituted by a building.

The second object of attack was historical determinism. Modern architecture, as propounded by its main theorists and historians, depended on a theory of history established in the early nineteenth century that, in part, interpreted cultural development through the metaphor of organic development. In this it was closely connected to the aesthetic theory of romanticism and its use of the organic analogy to explain the structure of artistic form. According to an extreme historicist interpretation, the cultural practice of any one period could be understood only from its position on an evolutionary time scale and as part of a causal-temporal chain. This approach was as vulnerable as that of functionalism to a structuralist critique. The countermodel was again Saussure's linguistics, an explication in terms of structure replacing one advanced in terms of linear causality.

Cultural systems—the argument goes—like language itself, can be explained less as temporal *processes* than as spatial structures. The cultural meanings of a period are interrelated, and the meaning of any one word, or any single artistic form, depends on the existence of all the others. If we take a practice like architecture, we can see that, as in the case of language, history is present not as a process in which each phase negates a previous one, but as a series of traces that survive in current ways of looking at the world. A historical form can therefore be seen as raw material *within* the present practice of architecture—not as something that has been relegated to an external past.

The application of the linguistic model to the arts resulted in a certain confusion, for it could be interpreted in one of two ways: as a syntactics that was "empty" or as a semantics that was "full." Neither of these interpretations contradicts the notion of the arbitrariness of the sign. Nor do they necesarily exclude each other, since one is concerned with the signifier and the other with the sign (signifier + signified) as its object of attention. But, I would argue, it is the second of these two interpretations that applies to architecture, a position best justified by Lévi-Strauss in his discussion of a different field—that of music.[3] Lévi-Strauss bases his argument on the analogy of the double articulations of language. In music, meaning (that is, "musical" meaning) is only imaginable if the sonic material has already been given a structure; new meanings can emerge only as modifications of an inherited structure. Now in music the basis for any such cultural structuration already exists in the natural degrees of dissonance. I would argue that a similar basis exists in architecture and that, therefore, architecture, like music, is both a natural and an arbitrary system.[4]

We can see from what I have said that structuralism was able to provide the rationale for an attack on two dogmas—functionalism and historical determinism—that were fundamental to the theory and practice of modernism. But structuralism could provide only a general critical framework. To understand how a structuralist critique might be applied to architecture requires a process of translation.

One means to such a translation is through the notion of type, which might explain how, within a system analogous to language, forms are generated in architecture. Just as language always preexists a group or individual speaker, the system of architecture preexists a particular period or architect. It is precisely through the persistence of earlier forms that the system can convey meaning. These forms, or *types*, interact with the tasks presented to architecture, in any moment in history, to form the entire system.

One of the many reasons why a typology of forms might have more impact on practice in architecture than in the other arts is the inherent reproducibility of architecture and its dependence on prototype. In the past, all the arts depended, to a greater or a lesser extent, on the faithful reproduction of prototypical elements. In classical artistic theory this use of prototypes was, so to speak, sublimated into the theory of mimesis, insofar as this applied to the imitation of models of classical art. The romantic movement condemned this concept as a denial of the absolute originality of each artwork; though the process was not destroyed, after romanticism it ceased to be a *de jure* practice and went underground. But in architecture the concept of reproducibility persisted. (It is curious that Benjamin does not mention this in his *Kunstwerk* essay.) Once an idea has been established in architecture it tends to be repeated in countless examples. Though monuments are seldom repeated exactly, more humble buildings like houses are often identical. This is no doubt partly because such buildings are intended to satisfy basic and continuing human needs, and partly because to translate an idea into material form requires the mediation of a number of agents, which in turn demands a certain degree of standardization.

All of which the modern movement understood. Both Hermann Muthesius and Le Corbusier made a connection between industrial production and an impersonal and normative classicism. The concepts of *Typisierung* and the *objet-type* were developed in the early days of the modern movement. But here the emphasis was on industrial production. The revival of the idea of type in the 1960s was certainly related to this aspect of modernism. But it differed from modernism in that it contained the notion of the repetition of certain morphologies in the history of architecture that appear to be independent of technical change. Giulio Carlo Argan, who revived this idea at a period of interest in Enlightenment architecture on the part of the *Casabella* group, based it on a rereading of the entry under "Type" in Quatremère de Quincy's *Dictionnaire historique d'architecture*. This notion of type has since become one of the recurrent ideas in the critical discourse of architecture.

In it we see an attempt to reinvest the form and body of a work of architecture with a dimension of meaning that depends on a kind of collective memory. The idea not only contests naive functionalism and the tyranny of technology over form; it also sets up a new kind of necessity in the place of function and historical determinism. It sets limits to the fancy of the architect and binds him to something analogous to the concept of *langue* in Saussure—a received structure and a collective possession that must be presupposed before any significance can be attributed to the *parole* of the individual speaker.

But in the notion of type, both as established by Quatremère and as reinterpreted by Argan and the *Casabella* group, there is a distinction between type and model. The reestablishment of continuity between modern architecture and history was the drive behind the whole concept, and it was supposed that this could be achieved by establishing an architectural typology at a relatively abstract level. But it has not proved so easy to distinguish between the abstract and the concrete, and it has, in practice, been impossible to distinguish absolutely between type and model.

Rather than try to give an account of all the different tendencies that, during the last ten years or so, have produced various fusions between traditional modernism and historical reference, and between a strict idea of typology and a free eclecticism, I would prefer to concentrate on a single problem: one that involves the relationship between a recovery of the past in architecture and an attitude toward social reality. I will here be concerned with architecture as affirmation or criticism.

The problem of distinguishing between an affirmative and a critical postmodernism is immediately complicated by uncertainty as to what aspect of cultural production is being attacked and what reinforced. If we examine modernism and the avant-garde as a necessary precondition for the discussion of postmodernism, we see that it is already fraught with ambiguities and reversals in this matter. In the dialectic of *Gemeinschaft* and *Gesellschaft* we find the seeds of most of these later ambiguities.[5] According to the proponents of *Gemeinschaft*, life in industrialized society was abstract and alienating.[6] But this implied an opposite interpretation: a true modern culture could not be achieved until we overcame our resistance to abstraction and specialization and were prepared to reject traditional values and their idealist underpinnings.

At the same time, the project of "modernization" stemming from the second interpretation of the *Gemeinschaft/Gesellschaft* opposition was itself imbued with an ideal content by architects like Muthesius and Le Corbusier. In a tendency related to the *rappel à l'ordre* in postwar Paris, the architecture of the machine age was seen as overcoming history to achieve a kind of transhistorical classicism. In an opposite movement, but still within this "progressivist" frame of mind, the *neue Sachlichkeit* architects called for the abandonment of all artistic pretensions in an architecture that would be absolutely objective and transparent to social needs.

Already, therefore, we can see the formation of a set of oppositions that becomes increasingly important: high art versus popular art; "modernization" as the symbol of artistic purity versus "modernization" as the symbol of social renewal.

There was an analogous situation in painting: a distinction can be made between on the one hand, a true "avant-garde" aiming at the subversion of the very concept of high art and, on the other, a "modernism" continuous with the historical development of the high artistic tradition (a position advocated by both Clement Greenberg and Theodor Adorno). A case in point is the argument between Adorno and Benjamin over "The Work of Art in the Age of Mechanical Reproduction." Benjamin perceived the cinema, in positive terms, as a new mass culture; Adorno condemned all mass culture as a symptom of cultural decadence—a decadence that it was the purpose of modernist art to arrest. Adorno's aesthetic theory is a typical reversal of the character traits of *Gemeinschaft* and *Gesellschaft*. Now a *Gesellschaft*-like abstractionism was identified with the preservation of culture, preventing art from being swallowed up by the culture industry. The autonomy of art, its aura, could only survive if the original conditions of its practice were abandoned.

If conflicts of this sort existed within modernism itself, those between the modernists and antimodernists in the interwar years were even more clear-cut. But they were cut along exactly the same cultural fault lines. In the 1930s, with the fading of postwar optimism in Russia and western Europe and with the rise of fascism, these conflicts became critical. The traditionalists surfaced in Germany, Italy, and Russia, promoting various forms of social realism. *Heimatstil* and state classicism in Germany, the projects of Marcello Piacentini in Mussolini's Rome, and the promotion of a "bourgeois" realism in Russia were closely related. And the same tendencies existed at the time in the democratic countries—notably in the United States.

After the war social realism continued in Russia; but in the West it was modernism that came to be associated with democracy and victory over fascism. In Germany and France, despite their many differences, a monolithic and professionalized modernism developed that made any external criticism virtually impossible. It was mainly in Italy that an external critique developed, due in part to the ambiguous relation of modernism to fascism, but also to the relative weakness of the institutional and financial structures, upon which large-scale housing and commercial development plans depended. This critique seems to have incoporated many influences, the chief of which was a new form of social realism—as found in the work of Ludovico Quaroni and Mario Ridolfi in Rome, whose housing projects borrowed formal elements from the vernacular tradition. In these tendencies we can perhaps discern the influence of Russian social realism and the artistic theories of Georg Lukács. At what point these various critical movements can be said to anticipate a "postmodernism" is doubtful and probably not very important. But postmodern or not, the attitudes of the subsequent movement of neorationalism—as represented, for example, by Aldo Rossi—constituted an unambiguous and uncompromising rejection of the doctrine of functionalism and opened the door to association and memory and to historical quotation. The simultaneous acceptance of some of the typical solutions of the 1920s by Rossi and Giorgio Grassi was not based on an acceptance of modernist dogma. Instead, they added certain modernist inventions to a more general typological inventory of architecture. The turning points of architectural history, represented by the Enlightenment and the earliest years of the modern movement, were approached with renewed interest as periods that could still provide analogies and models for the present situation. For the first time we see the project of revising the modern movement from a perspective that is no longer inside the modern movement itself.

It is interesting to note that the most coherent critique of modernism in Europe—that of the Italians—came from architects who belonged to the political left and were concerned with the fundamentally social role of architecture. It is true that the neorationalists stressed the relative autonomy of architecture and that they no longer considered architecture as capable of generating a technical, social, or political revolution. But this negative attitude toward architecture's revolutionary potential was not due to any desire to preserve the political status quo. Rather, it arose out of a loss of faith in technology as a liberating force, in the idea of "modernization," and in the corresponding elements of a modernist architecture.

What I am suggesting is that in this branch of postmodernism resides a theory of the work of architecture that contradicts the conflation that Adorno and the Frankfurt School made between modernism and cultural resistance. This new theory goes back to the notion of *Gemeinschaft* in the sense that it is critical of the increasing routinization and centralization of modern capitalist culture and sees in the autonomous tradition of architecture one way of combating this culture. It seems clear that this position combines a rather conservative concern for certain cultural traditions with a critique of modern capitalism: The affirmation of particular architectural "values" does not mean an endorsement of the existing political structure.

But it seems equally clear that the reintroduction of traditional stylistic elements and structures into contemporary architecture does not *in itself* mean anything at all. It does not necessarily imply either an affirmation of genuine architectural values or a criticism of modern cultural tendencies. What if the big corporations, increasingly the patrons of large architectural projects, go along with this change of architectural image? What if they see it merely as a change of fashion that can be easily accommodated within state-of-the-art technology and budgetary constraints? This, of course, is precisely what has happened. Architects who have been at the forefront of skyscraper development during the last thirty years have suddenly discovered that no economic (that is, functional) argument exists for a minimalist architecture deriving its expressive power from abstract geometry and a sleek, uniform curtain wall. Within reasonable limits, it is economically feasible to complicate the profile of a tall building in a number of different ways, including some that vaguely recall classical compositions.

To understand the contradiction between these two different examples of postmodern practice, we must return to the notion of type. A typology of forms that seeks to make available the more invariant elements of the historical tradition cannot ignore the problem of the program, however much it rejects function as the sole determinant of architecture. The use of historical forms implies some analogy—an analogy perhaps at the most general level—between the traditional uses associated with these forms and their present adaptation. Indeed, if, as the neorationalists claim, it is only through the manifestation of its autonomous codes that architecture can relate to social practice, this necessarily suggests, at some level, a homology between these codes and social practices.

If we look at the problem in this way we can see two poles limiting the use of historical motifs: at one pole, we find buildings whose purpose still bears some relation to a historically continuous *res publica*, or that are sited in dense, historically and artistically resonant urban contexts; at the other pole, we find new types without historical equivalence. The kind of postmodern practice associated with neorationalism often, though not invariably, fits into the first category. By contrast, the clearest examples of the second category are found in the forms of North America's predominant new building type, the corporate office building, whether low-spreading complexes in the countryside or towers in the city. Both programmatically and morphologically, this building type differs so greatly from any traditional type that when historical forms are applied to it, they operate in a kind of semantic void. These figures become merely the signs of "culture"; a previous signifier and signified have been collapsed and served up again as a new sign. The substance of the type remains stubbornly modern, while the building's clothing serves to give it a false appearance of architectural complexity and cultural depth. Such an interpretation is naturally very useful to a corporation eager to convince the public that it plays a responsible role in the realm of culture. Of course architecture has always been used in this way to "persuade," and whether such a rhetorical mode is acceptable or not is simply a question of one's position in a political spectrum. The problem that we encounter in the typical postmodern American office building is the lack of connection between the purpose of the building and the historical associations of its artistic form.

This situation seems to have been brought about by a cultural condition that is characteristically modern. During the last two hundred fifty years it has become increasingly possible to detach the aesthetic reception of works from the conditions of their creation. In his essay "The Modern System of the Arts," Paul Kristeller drew attention to the rise of amateur connoisseurship in the eighteenth century and the permanent shift this effected toward a receptionist theory of art.[7] The touchstone of artistic value was, he argued, no longer the artist or craftsman, but the spectator. This suggests a historically unique development since the eighteenth century; the "space of possibilities" of the artist and that of the spectator no longer coincide. The artist continues to be constrained by the technical and practical possibilities of his art, while the connoisseur is relatively free to adjust his threshold of perception to the art of different periods and different cultures.

This split between the artist and the spectator is an aspect of eclecticism seldom noticed. Eclecticism, which has usually been seen as something that exists equally for the artist and his audience, seems to be closely bound up with the increasing importance of connoisseurship. To take a counterexample, a period such as the sixteenth century reveals a general convergence between the artistic preoccupations of the artist and those of the public. When it becomes possible for cultivated people to enjoy the works of a historically remote culture, the forms of these works are immediately absorbed into artistic practice. For instance, the discovery of gesso decoration in the Domus Aurea in Rome inspired Raphael and others to revive both the techniques and the forms of this genre.

The distance between the space of possibilities of the spectator and of the artist has continued to grow. Some contemporary designers assume that the artist has the same access to the past as the connoisseur. But there seems no reason why a two-hundred-year trend in the opposite direction should suddenly be reversed. When artists go to museums, concert halls, or old cities, it is more in their capacity as connoisseurs than with the aim of learning how to operate a living tradition.

I began this paper with a claim for the importance of structuralism in the critique of modernist architecture. I would like to end it by pointing to the inadequacy of structuralism when the question is one of acting in a particular historical situation. Structuralism provides us with the field of possibilities that exists at any one moment; in doing so, it reintroduces the element of choice that was excluded by functionalism and historicism. But it remains silent about the motives for the choices that artists must continuously make—choices that, collectively, may determine the change from one set of paradigms to another.

No theory of architecture can ignore this problem. On the one hand, we must accept that there is no direct translation between function and form. Their relation is always mediated by custom and history. The architectural imagination should be free to choose from the entire cause of architectural forms without being constrained by *a priori* theories about the dictates of the spirit of the age. On the other hand, we should not think that this choice is unlimited. Architecture derives its meaning from the circumstances of its creation; and this implies that what is external to architecture—what can broadly be called its set of functions—is of vital importance. It is this that provides what Pierre Bourdieu has called the "motor." Structure and function are false opposites; they must be reconciled.

Notes

1 Andreas Huyssen, "Mapping the Post-modern," *New German Critique* 33 (Fall 1984): 5–52.

2 Walter Benjamin, "The Work of Art in the Age of Mechanical Reproduction," in *Illuminations*, trans. Harry Zohn (New York: Schocken Books, 1969), 239–40.

3 Claude Lévi-Strauss, *Le Cru et le cuit* (Paris, 1964); English ed., *The Raw and the Cooked: Introduction to a Science of Mythology I*, trans. John and Doreen Weightman (New York: Harper & Row, 1969).

4 See Alan Colquhoun, "Historicism and the Limits of Semiology," in *Essays in Architectural Criticism: Modern Architecture and Historical Change* (Cambridge: The MIT Press, 1981).

5 This typology originated with Ferdinand Tönnies, whose book *Gemeinschaft und Gesellschaft* of 1887 has had a lasting influence on sociological thought. *Gemeinschaft* and *Gesellschaft* are ideal types of association at the polar extremes of a continuum. In *Gemeinschaft*-like associations, relationships are spontaneous and affective and are ends in themselves. In *Gesellschaft*-like associations, on the contrary, relationships are the product of reason and calculation and are means to ends. The connection of this opposition to that between historicism, with its concept of an organic society, and Enlightenment rationalism, with its belief in natural law, is obvious. The two types are not thought of as mutually exclusive and both are held to exist in varying proportions in all societies.

6 This point of view can be seen most clearly in the early phase of romanticism, for example, in A. W. N. Pugin. The late-nineteenth-century German sociologists such as Tönnies and Georg Simmel were less prescriptive and more "scientific" in their approach. Thus in his discussion of the modern city in his essay "Die Grosstädte und das Geistesleben" (The Metropolis and Mental Life) of 1903, Simmel does not openly condemn the characteristic "abstract" and "nervous" quality of modern city life, despite his broad adherence to the school of *Lebensphilosophie* (translated in Kurt H. Wolff, ed., *The Sociology of Georg Simmel* [Glencoe, Ill.: Free Press of Glencoe, Illinois, 1950]).

7 Paul Oskar Kristeller, "The Modern System of the Arts," in *The Renaissance and the Arts: Collected Works*, rev. ed. (Princeton: Princeton University Press, 1980).

Illustration Credits

Page	Source
8	B. Seeley, *Stowe: A Description of the House and Garden* (1797).
10, 11	Robert Rosenblum, *Transformations in Late Eighteenth Century Art* (Princeton: Princeton University Press, 1967).
13	Nikolaus Pevsner, *Some Architectural Writers of the Nineteenth Century* (Oxford: Oxford University Press, 1972).
27	J. Fergusson, *Illustrated Handbook of Architecture* (1855).
29, top	J. J. Coulton, *Greek Artists at Work* (London: Granada, 1982).
37	Photograph by Alan Colquhoun.
38	© SPADEM, Paris. Courtesy Garland Publishing.
41, bottom	Arthur Drexler, *The Architecture of the Ecole des Beaux-Arts* (New York: Museum of Modern Art, 1977).
42	Arthur Drexler, *The Architecture of the Ecole des Beaux-Arts* (New York: Museum of Modern Art, 1977).
43, top	Georg Germann, *Gothic Revival in Europe and Britain* (Cambridge: The MIT Press, 1973).
43, bottom	Wolf Tegethoff, *Mies van der Rohe: The Villas and Country Houses* (New York: Museum of Modern Art, 1985).
44	Walter Gropius, *The New Architecture and the Bauhaus* (London, 1935).
53	© SPADEM, Paris. Courtesy Garland Publishing.
63	Staatliche Museen Preussischer Kulturbesitz, Kunstbibliothek mit museum für architectur, Modelbild und Grafik Design, Berlin.
68	*Das Abenteuer der Ideen: Architectur und Philosophie seit der Industriellen Revolution,* ed. Claus Baldus (Berlin: Internationale Bauausstellung, 1987).
70, 71	Centre d'histoire de la construction, Conservatoire nationale des arts et métiers, Paris.
78, top	Courtesy The Art Institute of Chicago.
78, bottom	Studio Terragni, Como.
80	Courtesy Paolo Libera, Rome.
82	*Das Abenteuer der Ideen: Architecktur und Philosophie seit der Industriellen Revolution,* ed. Claus Baldus (Berlin: Internationale Bauausstellung, 1987).
89–191	All the Le Corbusier illustrations are © SPADEM, Paris.

174	*Oeuvre complète,* vol. 2 (1929–34).
177, top	*Oeuvre complète,* vol. 2 (1929–34).
177, bottom	*Oeuvre complète,* vol. 3 (1934–38).
180	*Oeuvre complète,* vol. 3 (1934–38).
184, 185	*Oeuvre complète,* vol. 5 (1946–52).
186, top	*Oeuvre complète,* vol. 6 (1952–57).
186, bottom	Courtesy Garland Publishing.
188	*Oeuvre complète,* vol. 7 (1957–65).
189, top	*Oeuvre complète,* vol. 4 (1938–46).
189, bottom	*Oeuvre complète,* vol. 7 (1957–65).
194, 195	Leon Krier, *Rational Architecture* (Brussels: Archives d'architecture moderne, 1978).
203	Solomon D. Butcher Collection, Nebraska State Historical Society.
204	Luis Jesus Arizmendi Barnes, *Albert Speer. Arquitecto de Hitler: une Arquitectura Destruida* (Pamplona, Spain: EUNSA, 1978).
209	*Zodiac* 16 (1966).
210	Courtesy Foster Associates.
215, 216	*Oeuvre complète,* vol. 3 (1934–38). © SPADEM, Paris.
219, top	Paul Léon, *La Vie des monuments français: destruction, restauration* (Paris: Editions Picard, 1951.
219, bottom	Courtesy Kurt Forster.
220	Arthur Drexler, ed., *Tranformations in Modern Architecture* (New York: Museum of Modern Art, 1979).
228	Drawn by Cymbre Raub.

Page numbers of illustrations are in boldface

263